Build a Bridge . . . and Get Over It!

Build a Bridge . . . and Get Over It!

Dr. George H. Harris

Copyright © 2008 by Dr. George H. Harris.

Library of Congress Control Number: 2007908120
ISBN: Hardcover   978-1-4257-9897-0
               Softcover   978-1-4257-9892-5

All rights reserved. No part of this book may be reproduced or transmitted in any form or by any means, electronic or mechanical, including photocopying, recording, or by any information storage and retrieval system, without permission in writing from the copyright owner.

All Scripture quotations, unless otherwise indicated, are taken from the New King James Version of the Bible. © 1982 by Thomas Nelson, Inc.

This book was printed in the United States of America.

To order additional copies of this book, contact:
Xlibris Corporation
1-888-795-4274
www.Xlibris.com
Orders@Xlibris.com
44310

Contents

Chapter One: Destined To Be A Bridge Builder 9

Chapter Two: When Death Knocks And No One Answers 15

Chapter Three: Down, But Not Out 33

Chapter Four: The Perfect Storm 47

Chapter Five: The Danger Of Believing A Lie 56

Chapter Six: Blessings Unlimited 63

Chapter Seven: Put Your House In Order 73

Chapter Eight: Don't Quit Now 92

End Notes 103

This book is dedicated to Ann Harris (1945-2007), my quadrepeligic first cousin, whose life of adversity is a bridge to us all. Her positive optimism and surrender to the Lord Jesus has left everyone who knew her with a blueprint to build bridges over difficulty.

CHAPTER ONE

DESTINED TO BE A BRIDGE BUILDER

Choosing the Best

Years ago, I was just finishing a revival in my home church. My mother drove me to the airport in Little Rock, Arkansas to see me off. She gave me a big hug and then handed me a sealed envelope saying, "Honey, read this when you get on the plane. I wrote this letter to you ten years ago and it's been in safety deposit box for you to open at my death. However, I began to think something might happen to you before I die, and I wanted you to know about this letter. I was convinced I needed to give it to you now".

It wasn't long until the plane had reached altitude and the seat belt light had gone off that I remembered the letter in my pocket. As I began to read it, I was stunned; I couldn't have imagined in my wildest dreams the story that was contained therein.

The letter began:

> *Dear son, tonight I am so proud of you that I cannot sleep. Today, as I watched you walk across the stage and they conferred an Honorary Doctors Degree on you, pride filled my heart in ways that I cannot explain. You are a fulfillment of my dream and my life. What I'm about to tell you, you would never know.*
>
> *In 1933, I was a young seventeen-year-old girl. Your father and I fell in love and secretly married. Three years before, I had surrendered my life to foreign missions and felt that God would have me go and be a missionary, but as fate would have it, I fell in love with your father. In those days during the depression we had very little money. We couldn't afford to live on our own, so we married without anyone knowing it.*
>
> *It wasn't long until I found out that I was pregnant with you. I did not know what I was going to do. I was so afraid. I went to three different doctors in the town and around the county seeking an abortion. But in those days, doctors were reluctant to perform abortions, so my attempts failed.*
>
> *Eventually you were born, and I came to the realization that I would never be able to fulfill my commitment to the Lord as a missionary. Your dad was not aware of my decision, nor was he sympathetic with me ever being a missionary. Several months later, when you were eighteen months old and I was pregnant with your sister, you were playing out on*

the back porch and I looked through the window onto the back porch and saw you playing. The sunrays were coming through the glass shining on your face. You looked almost angelic. Such joy filled my heart because you had become the very joy of my life. I dried my hands on my apron and walked out and knelt down by you. I picked you up and set you on my knees and on the back porch that day with the sun beams coming ever so gently through the window, I turned my voice heavenward and pledged you to God. I said, 'Lord, I will be the handmaid of this boy. I want him to be your servant and to serve in my place'.

From that day forth I have pledged you to Him. I never told you this all of these years. Even when you were struggling with the call to the ministry and your dad was unsympathetic, I did not tell you because I did not want you to feel obligated to surrender to the ministry because of any pressure that I may have put upon you. But today as you walked across that stage, I looked back over the years. You brought me great joy and you have been an extension of what I would have wanted my life to be. I love you very much.

Mother

I can't begin to tell you what this 40-year-old man was feeling in his heart seated on that airplane alone that night. Everything that I had ever accomplished up to that moment in my life, I realized, had been almost predestined and foreordained by God and a godly mother who had always been praying for me. She had chosen the best of the options that had been given her. The doctors that had refused to accommodate her with the bad option of abortion had, in reality, extended her life and brought her great blessings. Choosing the best option is the way you build a bridge in the midst of crisis.

*   *   *

It was December 7, 1941. Pearl Harbor had just been bombed and the Second World War was in full swing. I can remember walking home from school mid-afternoon one day in May. My report card was hidden in my backpack, and as I trudged toward home, I wondered how my mom was going to take it. On the back of the card read the words, "REPEAT THE THIRD GRADE." I had failed! My dad was miles away in Navy boot camp in California, and my mom was working at a local furniture company in our little town.

You see, my war was just beginning. Rather than going back to repeat the third grade, I was enrolled in Mrs. Frankie's Retarded Children's School. It was nothing more than six or seven school desks in her living room in an old house. This was the place they put "slow" kids, kids who weren't reading very well or children that were affected with some kind of physical defect such as Cerebral Palsy and other diseases or infirmities. I had no idea what I was doing there. I was perfectly normal in appearance and didn't seem to be getting anywhere in the school; instead, I came home at the close of the day mimicking the deformities of the children around me. It was obvious after about six months that the school was doing me more harm than good. Eventually I was put back in public school. From then on, it was pass a grade, fail a grade, pass a grade, and fail a grade, until I finally managed to graduate high school after attending summer school almost every summer in order to pass.

It wasn't until I was 30 years old and a graduate of college and seminary that I discovered, quite by accident, what my problem was: I was a dyslexic. I had an eye muscle coordination problem. No one in 1940 knew what that was, or even what to call it, and much less how to treat it. Now, years later, I was pastor of the county seat First Baptist Church. A sweet lady in my church, who was working on her P.H.D. in childhood education, discovered my problem.

It was suspected that dyslexia was caused by one of three things: either by heredity from the father, by high fever in infancy, or by skipping the crawling stage as a baby. I had two of the conditions present in my history for sure, and possibly the third. My father only finished the eighth grade, but was a genius in math. He could figure in his head faster than most people could figure on paper, but he never could tell you how he got the answer. He could not work algebra equations but he could always give you the correct answer. I always suspected that he was a dyslexic. Also, I had the measles when I was three weeks old and ran a high fever for several days. And, yes, I skipped the crawling stage and, as a result, never developed eye-hand coordination. I had all of the major causes as suspected by those who were studying the cause of dyslexia.

What a relief to discover that I was not stupid; that I had something that could be treated! That lady took me on as a special project unknown to anyone else in my church. My first assignment was to crawl. That's right—crawl—for thirty minutes every day! I hope you can imagine what a humbling experience this was for a 30-year old pastor with two children. Each day after lunch I would return to my study. I would tell my secretary not to disturb me, that I would be studying. Then with the door locked, I would get down on my hands and knees and crawl around the room for thirty minutes. There were other coordination exercises, but this was the most memorable one. You might say this was building a bridge. No one will ever know what this did for me. It was a bridge of confidence, courage and a challenge to go on. I re-enrolled in seminary in 1969 and eight years later, graduated with the Doctor of Ministries Degree. Looking back over the years, I realize many men had this same problem: Ted Bundy, the notorious serial killer, John D. Rockefeller and Winston Churchill to mention three. All of these had extremely high IQ's. Some built bridges and got over it, and some let it destroy them.

No one builds bridges by themselves. In college, my wife would read English Literature and World History and then tell me what it was all about. She read my Greek lessons to me in the car as we drove back from our weekend church. I made A's and B's and graduated as a result of her patience and commitment to me. I will always be indebted to a couple of men: Dr. Joe T. McClain, my Greek professor; and Dr. Robert G. Whitte my seminary professor when I was working on my Doctor of Ministries Degree. Their encouragement to me during these days of bridge building will never be forgotten.

We not only need to be bridge builders, but we need to teach others how to do the same.

CHAPTER TWO

WHEN DEATH KNOCKS AND NO ONE ANSWERS

On a cold Saturday morning in November, 2002, nine of my friends and I planned a motorcycle ride through the Texas Hill Country. I had arranged to meet the other nine at the busy intersection of IH-10 and Highway 46 in Boerne. Each of the riders showed up as scheduled at around seven o'clock in the morning, and after our regular greetings and small talk, we set off for a perfect, scenic ride in the cool autumn air.

We stopped in the small town of Bandera along the way for coffee and conversation, and then began our ride to Frio County, where we planned to eat lunch before our return home. The outing promised to be the experience of a lifetime! The entire trip would take a few hours round trip and would take us along winding rural roads, hills and valleys neatly tucked away from the hustle of San Antonio, and spectacular views that would take one's breath away.

It was a perfect ride for someone like me, who had not ridden a motorcycle for fifteen years. Though rusty, not to mention the oldest man in the group, I was determined not to let anything interfere with the euphoric feeling that came with the rushing wind through my helmet and the roar of those Harley pipes. It was a feeling that most men crave, whether openly or in secret: the feeling of independence, freedom, and adventure.

We arrived at our lunch destination in the rural town of Leakey well before noon and ate our lunch at a local diner. I was finally beginning to thaw out as we were leaving the cafe. Although the temperature was relatively mild—thirty-nine degrees—the hour-and-a-half ride in the open wind had chilled me to the bone. Most of me had warmed up a little during lunch, but my face still felt numb and frozen. Because I had no covering for my face, the wind chill had taken its toll on my face, which was the only part of my body with skin exposed. After we paid for our meal and returned to our bikes to begin our journey home, one of the younger men in the group, whom I had known since he was a toddler, called out to me.

"Hey, Preacher, put this on!" He tossed me a ski mask. I appreciated the gesture very much and promptly put on the ski mask, then strapped my helmet on over it.

It was time to be off, so I mounted my bike and started it up. The first three riders in the group had already taken off, and by the time I was settled in and ready to go, they were at least seventy-five yards ahead. I knew I was holding up the other riders who would be following behind me. I had to catch up. I quickly took off, shifted into second gear, and gunned it, attempting to make up for lost time.

Then, the unexpected happened: as I was rapidly approaching the others, I saw the brake lights of all three bikes ahead of me turn on simultaneously. They had come to a dead stop. I was approaching them quickly and needed to stop, and fast.

I instantly hit the brake, but in my haste, I forgot to squeeze the hand brake, and the bike went into a sudden and unrecoverable skid. I struggled to keep the heavy machine upright to no avail. The bike skidded across the double yellow line in the highway and began careening towards the guardrail in the oncoming lane.

I saw a cliff on the other side of that guard rail that dropped off at least fifty feet, and I had a split-second decision to make: I could either go over the cliff with the bike, or I could lay the bike down right there in the road and attempt to step off while traveling at my current speed of forty-five miles per hour. I opted for the second choice.

Whether or not I made the best decision in those brief moments, no one will ever know. As I put my left foot on the ground and lifted my right leg over the bike to dismount, the momentum of the bike immediately catapulted my body straight up in the air. I was moving so quickly that before I could even think to put my hands in front of me to break my fall, I smashed into the pavement; face first, my nose making the initial contact with the cold, hard asphalt.

Oddly, the impact did not knock me unconscious. I sat up, dazed and shaken. My first thought was, "Man, that hurt!" I sat there in the road for a few seconds, trying to gather my wits. The young man riding directly behind me, a San Antonio police officer and former EMS medic named Eric, pulled up and quickly rushed to my side.

Eric swiftly helped me off of the highway and propped me up against the guardrail. He then carefully peeled the ski mask off my face, which immediately revealed the gravity of the situation.

Blood began to gush from my mouth and nose. I quickly realized that I could not close my mouth. I would find out later that my jaw was broken and my upper palate was crushed in several places, and sitting there on the pavement, I could feel my teeth pushing awkwardly back into my mouth at an angle. I had double vision because the force of the impact had shattered both of my eye sockets, and my left eye, without bone to hold it into my skull, hung precariously out of place.

The men in the group called 911. The local police showed up and began to ask me questions about the accident, which I could not answer due to my condition.

After what seemed like an eternity, the EMS arrived, and the tech on duty ran towards me to assess the situation. He immediately determined that I was too critical to be moved by ambulance, so he summoned Air Rescue.

I only remember short snatches after that: the whirl of the helicopter blades fanning me as I lay on the stretcher, the pilot reassuring me by saying, "We're almost there," landing at University Hospital and hearing the attendant say to the pilot, "Hurry, or we're going to lose him." In the fog that had descended over my mind, I thought that they were talking about some other passenger on the helicopter. I could not fathom my critical condition. "Strange," I thought. "I don't remember them taking on another patient." Then my world went black.

I found out later that when the helicopter touched down, I went into respiratory arrest. The trauma to my face and throat had shut down my breathing. The ER technicians performed an emergency tracheotomy and, after several critical minutes of work, they restored my breathing.

I then underwent a series of endless tests to assess the damage wrought on my body. The tests revealed that I had a skull fracture. Though no evidence of any other bodily injuries existed—not even road rash!—every bone in my face was shattered because my face absorbed the full impact of the crash.

My wife, Lynda, and my children rushed to the hospital as soon as they received the news of the accident. When they saw me for the first time, they did not recognize me. The massive bruising left my face and head bright purple, and my face was swollen beyond belief. They remained with me day and night, taking turns at my bedside, as I lay unconscious.

The news about my accident circulated quickly as the local media reported the details of my condition. Hundreds of friends, church members, past and present, and even total strangers called, visited, and prayed. The whole city of San Antonio became aware of the event and of my current state.

After spending several days in the University Hospital trauma center, my family consulted with Dr. Steven Buckley of Alamo Maxillofacial Surgeons. He immediately had me transferred to nearby Methodist Hospital for surgery. Dr. Buckley and his partners assured my family that they could reconstruct my face and repair the massive damage. They requested close-up pictures of my face—front views as well as profile pictures—so that they could gain an accurate perspective of how I looked prior to my crash.

(Lynda recovered her sense of humor in the midst of the crisis and offered the doctors several pictures of Tom Cruise. Obviously the surgery failed, because I still came out looking like George Harris in the end!)

After eight hours of reconstructive surgery, I awoke with my jaw wired shut. I had a feeding tube in my side as well as a brace on my nose. The surgeons had placed eleven titanium plates, two orbital implants, and eighty-seven screws in my face.

The next three months of convalescence were the most difficult of the whole ordeal. I couldn't speak because my mouth was wired closed, and for the greater portion of the time, I could not see to read. Other complications sent me back for laser surgery to open my throat because the forced tracheotomy had caused my airway to constrict by about 75%.

Depression set in and I wanted to die. I had to depend on my family constantly. My tracheotomy tube had to be suctioned and the feeding tube regularly replenished, the duties of which fell upon Lynda. I couldn't sleep most nights because the antibiotics, steroids, and decongestants kept me awake.

Because I could not lie down to sleep, I sat up in a recliner chair almost every night, and because I could not sleep, I prayed. One night, completely at the end of myself, I called out to God in desperation and asked Him to let me die if things were going to continue like they were. The depression caused me to lose sight of all hope and faith, and in spite of all the care and encouragement from hundreds of cards and calls, flowers and food, I dwelt in darkness as never before.

At this moment, alone in the recliner, God led me to the 116th Psalm, and in the silent night, I discovered Him in a way I had never known Him before. In that deeply despondent moment, I read Psalm 116 with my magnifying glass, painstakingly taking it word by word the best I could with my eyes still healing. Though it seemed by chance that I had stumbled onto that particular Psalm, I now know it was not by chance, but a "God-thing," because He had a special message just for me. Keep in mind that I had visited death's door several times during the past weeks—on the roadway, in a helicopter, and then in the intensive care rooms. The words of the Psalmist seemed to be written just for me:

> *I love the LORD, because He has heard*
> *My voice and my supplications.*
> *Because He has inclined His ear to me,*
> *Therefore I will call upon Him as long as I live.*
> (Psalm 116:1-2)

As I read the opening lines to the Psalm, the Lord Jesus visited me in a very personal way. Though I could not open my mouth, I could still speak to Him in my heart. And through His word and by His Spirit, He spoke back to me. My lonely suffering became an awesome encounter as the words of the Psalmist became a *word* (rhema[1]) to me personally. This Psalm is indeed a word for anyone suffering. I continued reading:

> *The pains of death surrounded me,*
> > *And the pangs of Sheol laid hold of me;*
> > *I found trouble and sorrow.*
> *Then I called upon the name of the LORD:*
> > *"O LORD, I implore You, deliver my soul!"*
>
> *Gracious is the LORD, and righteous;*
> > *Yes, our God is merciful.*
> *The LORD preserves the simple;*
> > *I was brought low, and He saved me.*
> *Return to your rest, O my soul,*
> > *For the LORD has dealt bountifully with you.*
>
> *For You have delivered my soul from death,*
> > *My eyes from tears,*
> > *And my feet from falling.*
> *I will walk before the LORD*
> > *In the land of the living.*
> *I believed, therefore I spoke,*
> > *"I am greatly afflicted."*
> *I said in my haste,*
> > *"All men are liars."*

What shall I render to the LORD
For all His benefits toward me?
I will take up the cup of salvation,
And call upon the name of the LORD.
I will pay my vows to the LORD
Now in the presence of all His people.

Precious in the sight of the LORD
Is the death of His saints.

O LORD, truly I am Your servant;
I am Your servant, the son of Your maidservant;
You have loosed my bonds.
I will offer to You the sacrifice of thanksgiving,
And will call upon the name of the LORD.

I will pay my vows to the LORD
Now in the presence of all His people,
In the courts of the LORD's house,
In the midst of you, O Jerusalem.

Praise the LORD!
(Psalm 116:3-19)

These nineteen verses came alive as though they were written for me. I know I had read them before, but suddenly the message was not about David and his near death experience, but about me. In fact, I could have written the Psalm had David not penned it hundreds of years earlier. I began to study the verses one by one, and they became my Psalm as God gave each verse to me, personally.

Out of that blessed silence came much-needed words from God's heart to mine, and ultimately, came this book.

That glorious night, I discovered five things I want to share with you.

THE DECLARATION

> *"I love the Lord because He has heard my voice and my supplications. Because He has inclined His ear to me, therefore I will call upon Him as long as I live." (Psalm 116:1-2)*

The first two verses of Psalm 116 set forth my declaration, which was the same as David's. The Hebrew word *shama* is translated "hear" and it means, "to hear intelligently (with attention or obedience) ². God certainly heard my cry. I declared with David "to call upon the Lord as long as I live." The Hebrew word *yowm* used here means "continually."

In the dark and silent night, I made a declaration to God that I would love Him in a way that I had never loved Him before. All other interests seemed to vanish. The sense of His presence was so great, and I was not interested in preaching sermons or achieving denominational prominence. All other endeavors seemed anticlimactic in the great and awesome presence of the Lord.

I vowed that night that I would no longer take engagements to preach, but instead, I would take only assignments from Him. I would go only where He sent me. In the time since I had retired from my pastorate in June till the accident in November, I had become tired of going from church to church merely "filling the pulpit," business as usual. I preached old sermons that were becoming stale to me even though people seemed to like them. I felt little more than a performer "doing my gig" and going home.

As I sat in the darkness in my living room, swaddled in the presence of the Lord, I knew there had to be more. I would no longer be satisfied. God wanted more from me, and He wanted to do more than I was allowing Him to do. I declared that night that if He let me live to preach again, I would not sink to the level of mediocrity with which I had become content.

THE DANGER

> *"The pains of death encompassed me, and the pangs of Sheol laid hold of me: I found trouble and sorrow." (Psalm 116:3)*

As I continued to read the Psalm, I realized just how much my condition was like the one David described. The word "sorrow" is translated in the Hebrew as *habl*, which means "to travail, to labor in childbirth." David is saying of his experience, "I was in the troughs of giving birth to death." That had been my experience exactly! I felt that I had been rescued from the jaws of Sheol (the place of the departed dead).

> *"Then I called upon the name of the Lord: 'O Lord, I implore You, deliver my soul!'" (Psalm 116:4)*

The Hebrew word for soul, *nephesh*, is used three times and means "to refresh oneself." The Hebrew Greek Study Bible notes, "The derivate noun appears to denote breath."[3] I had lost my breath as the helicopter was landing. The attempt to restore my breathing by inserting a tube into my throat had failed, and unless something drastic was done, and quickly, death was imminent. I am told that the ER surgeon performed a forceful tracheotomy to restore my breathing and God literally restored my soul.

THE DISCOVERY

"Gracious is the Lord, and righteous; yes, our God is merciful." (Psalm 116:6)

Though it was not immediately evident, I discovered in the months to come just how gracious the Lord continued to be. The words "gracious," "righteous," and "merciful" all took on a deeper meaning. The word *chanan*, translated "gracious," means "to be favorable, to be in negotiation with."[4]

Sometimes we take God's three attributes—graciousness, righteousness, and mercy—for granted. God's unmerited favor upon me was certainly evident that day on the highway. I didn't deserve to live any more than some folks who died that same day in other places. Why me, Lord? Obviously, He had other plans. Righteousness is a term I don't totally understand to this day because of my unrighteousness as a human being. I have a hard time understanding the quality that only God possesses fully.

I do understand mercy. Someone defined mercy as "that which we don't receive even though we deserve it," while grace is "God giving us what we do not deserve." I certainly did not deserve the kindness of God poured out on me in the days after the accident. The manifold grace of God was revealed through human kindness in so many ways that it stretches me to describe them.

One memorable experience came at a time I doubted that I had any usefulness left in my future. A man over six feet tall came into my room and knelt down beside my bed. He stretched out his hand and introduced himself.

"You don't remember me, do you?" he asked. I didn't. He paused.

"Do you remember, back in 1985, talking to a fellow in a Corvette in a parking lot across from the Denim and Diamonds club?" I vaguely remembered this meeting.

He went on to tell me that he had been sitting in his car in the parking lot when I came out of Whataburger, which was across the street from the nightclub he mentioned. I couldn't help but admire the bright new Corvette, and I walked over and complimented him on his car. He said, "That night in the parking lot, you told me about Jesus, and I prayed to receive Christ."

"What you didn't know," he continued, "was that as we talked, I had a 357 Magnum in my lap. I was despondent and depressed, and I had made up my mind to drive out on the highway and end it all. You saved my life, and I have never thanked you."

I was stunned at his story. I listened intently as he concluded:

"When I heard you were in the hospital, I felt that I needed to let you know how God used you that night. I am the Minister of Missions on the staff of a local church. Had it not been for your faithfulness, I wouldn't be here now."

He prayed for me, and then he left. I have not seen him since, but his visit was a reminder that each of us can be an instrument of grace and mercy, and that God has a way of extending His righteousness through us. His visit came when I needed it most.

THE DECISION

"The Lord preserves the simple; I was brought low, and He saved me. Return to your rest, O my soul, for the Lord has dealt bountifully with you. For you have delivered my soul from death, my eyes from tears, and my feet from falling. I will walk before the Lord in the land of the living." (Psalm 116:6-9)

These verses expressed the decision I made that night. The words in verse seven were a direct word from God to me. I could return to my rest, assured that God was not finished with me and that He was definitely up to something. He had certainly dealt bountifully with me. He spelled it out in sermonic fashion:

> He had delivered my soul from death.
> He had delivered my eyes from tears.
> He had delivered my feet from falling.

How much more specific could that have been? I affirmed with the Psalmist "to walk in the land of the living." From now on, I would look at things through different eyes. It had never occurred to me how special God's children are to Him. I was so absolutely overcome; His love and care for me were beyond description.

But soon the ecstasy of the moment passed, and I, like the Psalmist, said with great despondency:

"I believed, therefore I spoke, 'I am greatly afflicted.' I said in my haste, 'All men are liars.' What shall I render to the Lord for all His benefits toward me? (vs.10-12)

Notice the question mark at the end of the sentence. I, like the Psalmist, felt total despair when I realized I had no way of paying God back for all He had done for me. Then, it dawned on me that God did not expect me to pay Him back. All He wanted from me was my adoration.

"I will take up the cup of salvation." The words "take up" or "lift up" means "to raise." The Psalmist is saying, "I will praise God for all He is doing or has done. That is what He wants, nothing more." In verse 14 we read these words, "What is the difference in paying a vow and in taking a vow?"

This idea came to me. In 1956 my wife and I stood before a minister and exchanged our wedding vows. "Do you promise to love him/her and cherish him/her in that relationship, in sickness and in health, in riches and in poverty, 'till death do you part?" We both said, "I do." That was "taking the vows." Now, nearly fifty years later, as Lynda cared for me night after night, suctioning the tube in my throat when it became clogged, filling the feeding tube, giving me my endless medications, cleaning and bandaging my incisions, even rushing me to the emergency room at three o'clock in the morning on two occasions, holding me close and encouraging me when I was so despondent . . . that, my dear friend, is "paying your vows."

It is a lot easier to take the vows than to pay them. Years before, when I was an eight-year-old boy, I had taken a vow to become a Christian. I stood before a congregation at the end of Vacation Bible School and professed my faith in Jesus Christ. I had made a vow to be His child and to follow Him. Now, it came to me that following Jesus is more than taking a vow. It means, as the Psalmist put it, "I will pay my vow in the presence of all His people." It means that you must live out what you pledge. So many of us have taken vows but have never paid them. It became so clear to me in those days that Lynda cared for me. She could have hired someone to do those thankless tasks; she could have deserted me and made excuses, but she paid the vows that she had taken 45 years earlier.

Jesus is looking for followers that will not only take a vow, but who will also pay their vows in the sanctuary, in the presence of the people.

THE DISCOVERY AND THE GREAT DOXOLOGY

"Precious in the sight of the Lord is the death of His saints." (Psalm 116:15)

I had used this verse at funerals, but I had never used it in the context of the Psalm. Charles Spurgeon, the great English preacher of the 1800's, says of this verse that God is so interested in His saints that at death He shows up to take them home. The Psalmist is saying that we are never out of His sight.

At this point, David breaks out into a praise doxology:

"I will offer to You the sacrifices of thanksgiving, and will call upon the name of the Lord. I will pay my vows to the Lord now in the presence of all His people, in the courts of the Lord's house, in the midst of you, O Jerusalem. Praise the Lord!" (Psalm 116:17-19)

I am not the only person to whom God has revealed Himself in crisis situations. I am only one of many. I am sure of one thing, though: God wants us to encourage each other with our experiences.

A few months after my wreck, I traveled to Kansas City to attend a trustee meeting at Midwestern Baptist Seminary, where I served on the board of trustees. As I sat down on my return flight, I noticed a man boarding the airplane who was carrying a large trophy. To my surprise, he sat down in the seat right next to me.

He introduced himself as Herman Morris. I introduced myself and then complimented him on his trophy. He said, "Oh, it's not mine. It belongs to my son. We were in Kansas City for an awards banquet last night and are headed back to San Antonio."

"Who is your son?" I asked.

"Priest Holmes," he replied. "He plays with the Kansas City Chiefs."

I did not recognize the name, but I said, "Well, my son probably knows him. My son is the sports anchor for Channel 4 in San Antonio."

"Sure! I know Don!" the man exclaimed. "He has interviewed my son, and we have talked on the phone with Don several times!"

He paused, and then added, "You were in a bad wreck not too long ago, weren't you?"

I told him the short version of my story, and, to my amazement, he then told me a story that topped mine!

In 1998, Herman was working at Kelly Air Force Base in San Antonio. He was in a hangar working in the cockpit of a B52 with another man when a fire ignited beneath the plane. He opened the cockpit door to flee, and then realized that the fuselage was completely engulfed in flames. Some of the other workers who were working farther back in the plane were trapped and could not escape through the rear exit. Herman quickly shut the cockpit door, leaving him and his partner trapped in the cockpit with no means of escape.

Herman panicked as the smoke began to fill the cockpit. He could hear the shouts of the men in the back of the plane as they fought to escape. He was desperate. He was running out of air. Suddenly, he heard a voice that said, "The window is your only way out!" Herman knew that jumping out of the cockpit window meant plunging two stories to the pavement below, but he had no choice.

"The window! We have to jump," he shouted to his friend.

They both ran to the window and looked down. The floor below was an inferno.

"We can't jump!" his friend shouted. "It's just as bad down there!"

Herman looked again and noticed a small clearing on the floor not too far from where he would land if he jumped. He decided to go for it. He tried to urge his friend to do the same, but his friend, fearful, refused.

I held my breath as Herman continued:

"I took a deep breath, mustered all of my strength, and kicked out the window. I had to squeeze through the tiny space—the windows on those planes are not large enough to accommodate a person—and I climbed out onto the nose of the airplane. I was scared to death when I looked down at the floor so far below, but I felt I had no choice, so I jumped.

"When I landed in the flames, I began to roll toward the space I had seen that was clear of the fire. I broke both ankles on impact and was on fire when I reached the space. I somehow managed to extinguish the flames on my body, and the last thing I remember was glancing up to see my coworkers perishing in the fire above me."

He finished his story by saying, "Preacher, I learned a great lesson in life through that experience. Sometimes the only way out is through the fire, and if that is the way God takes you, then you had better go."

Herman told me that he spent a good part of the next two years recovering from his burns and injuries. He said that he is now the member of a local congregation, where he sings in a gospel quartet and travels, "paying his vows to the Lord." My eyes were filled with tears as I sat awestruck by what I had just heard.

As the plane landed, a handsome young man walked up the aisle and said, "Dad, I'll carry that trophy for you." Herman introduced me to his son, Priest, and we exchanged pleasantries and then parted ways.

The Lord taught me a valuable lesson that day through Herman: sometimes the only way out is through the fire, and when God delivers us, we must not fail to tell the story. I decided that day that I do not want a trophy—I want to be a trophy. David said it best: "I will pay my vows to the Lord, now in the presence of all His people."

Build a bridge with your testimony!

CHAPTER THREE

DOWN, BUT NOT OUT

From the pages of the Old Testament comes one of the most touching stories ever written. This drama is tucked away in the history recorded in 1 and 2 Samuel. Unless we read the Bible with a critical eye, chances are that we will miss one of the greatest pictures of God's grace in all of Scripture. Reading from 1 Samuel 17 to 2 Samuel 9, we find the dynasty of King Saul as he rules, reigns, dies, and then passes the kingdom to his successor, King David. It is a saga that is a match for any modern-day story of suspense, sex, love, and war.

Often missed in these chapters is the relationship between Saul's son, Jonathan, and the shepherd/soldier, David. The young men were closer-than-brother best friends, about whom the Scriptures say, "Each loved the other as himself." After David's many victories leading the armies of Israel, Saul became jealous of him and his popularity with the people.

Saul felt that David was a threat to his kingdom, and David sensed that Saul wanted to kill him.

Jonathan was not convinced, but together, David and Jonathan devised a scheme to force Saul to reveal his heart toward David. The plot, laid out in 1 Samuel 19 and 20, proved without a doubt that Saul was, indeed, planning to kill David. Before David fled for his life, he and Jonathan made a covenant that they would take care of each other, and in the event of the death of one or the other, the one remaining would care for the other's heirs.

David and Jonathan parted ways, never to see each other again, and David became a fugitive from the wrath of Saul. As the events unfolded, King Saul died at his own hand and Jonathan was killed in battle, making way for David to become Israel's king. In 2 Samuel 9, we are introduced to Jonathan's heir, a son named Mephibosheth, who became crippled by a fall as a child when his nurse dropped him as they fled from the battle.

In those days, there was really no way a crippled man could make a living. He couldn't work and he couldn't go into military service, so he was completely at the mercy of others. We're not sure of the details surrounding Mephibosheth, but it is written that he lived in the house of Machir, the son of Ammiel, in Lo Debar. It is suspected that this Machir was probably a relative of Bathsheba since she had a brother by that name. It is also probable that Mephibosheth was a very degenerate person due to his circumstances, though this cannot be proven. He referred to himself as "a dead dog," and this term was used for male prostitutes in Deuteronomy 23:18. At best, Mephibosheth saw himself as no better than a dead animal, and at worst, he was a temple prostitute to earn a living.

At any rate, he is seen as a hopeless piece of humanity, falling short of fulfilling the life for which he had been intended. Nevertheless, David rescued him and restored to him all that had belonged to his fathers, mainly the kingdom wealth of Israel. By this time, David owned everything from Lebanon to Egypt and from the Mediterranean Sea to Persia. In short, David kept the covenant made with his friend Jonathan and saw to it that Mephibosheth was heir to all that had been his father's.

The story of Mephibosheth is a story of a person who was down, but not out. What a great lesson to apply to us as believers. We, too, are often down, but we are never out. There are circumstances that set us back, there are moments of depression that leave us despondent, but as the Lord's children, we are heirs to all that is His. According to Romans 8:17 and Romans 8:28, we are heirs and joint-heirs with Jesus. God is working all things out for our good if we are indeed in His family. No matter how long we may have sunk into sin and degradation, no matter how guilt-ridden we may be, we are heirs and we are never beyond the redeeming love of the King who is in search for us.

WE ARE THE OBJECT OF THE KING'S SEARCH

David came looking for anyone who belonged to the house of Jonathan. Mephibosheth had been a cripple for years.[1]

Have you thought about the covenant God made with His Son to redeem a people for Himself in the morning hours of redemption before the foundation of the world? He chose the nation of Israel to be His special people, and now He has chosen the church, the body of Christ, and all who will confess Him as Savior. To many as believe on His name, they become the children of God.

Just as David came looking for Jonathan's heir[2], so the Lord Jesus came looking for us.

Bound by a covenant

Just as David made a covenant to care for Jonathan's heirs twenty years or more before he found Mephibosheth, God has an everlasting covenant with His Son to redeem the fallen sons of mankind. David never forgot the covenant he made that day in the field and the duty that was his to carry out.

Sought by a command

When Jesus left this earth, He gave a command to the church to go into all the world and make disciples.[3] We call this the Great Commission, and we have been carrying out this command for over two thousand years. Jesus said, "I have come to seek and to save that which is lost."[4]

When David came looking for Mephibosheth, he asked, "Is there someone of the house of Saul to whom I may show the kindness of God?"[5] Ziba, the servant, pointed the king to the so-called "down-and-outer," Mephibosheth. Like Mephibosheth, we were all down and out in sin when Christ found us. Jesus came "to seek and to save that which was lost."[6]

Found for a purpose

The king had a purpose for Mephibosheth—not only to prove his loyalty to Jonathan, but also to restore a member of the royal family. Mephibosheth was never intended to be living like an indigent . . . he was royalty! In like manner, God has a purpose for each of us. Even though sin has taken its toll in our lives because we were crippled by Adam's fall, there is hope! We are the very objects of the King's search. His mission is to make us into His image so that we may live in communion with Him as one of the King's sons[7]. Paul wrote in Romans: "We are heirs of God and joint-heirs with Christ[8]."

The purpose for which we have been found is to let Christ live His royal life through us. Yes, we are crippled and lame on both of our spiritual feet, but we have been raised up to sit in heavenly places, to reign in His strength. While Mephibosheth could not till the land or serve his country, David provided servants for him. In the same way, God has provided the Holy Spirit to work in us to allow us to live above our normal carnal strengths. We would all be failures in the Christian life were it not for Christ living in us in the presence of the Holy Spirit. His life in us is our hope of glory[9].

WE ARE SUBJECT TO THE KING'S WISH

More than anything, God wants us to know Him and to know His heart regarding His children. There are so many foreign ideas about God. Some people see Him as the Judge who waits to sentence us when we are caught in sin. Others see Him as the one so far removed that we can never know Him. Both views are far from the true heart of God, which is revealed in the classic illustration of the story of Mephibosheth.

The King's wish is to know us personally

Notice that when King David sent for Mephibosheth, he did not call Him by a number, nor did he say, "Hey, you!"

He referred to him by name. In that same way, God wants us to have a personal relationship with Him. Knowing the king personally was a hard concept for Mephibosheth to perceive because he felt his unworthiness so acutely. Had he realized who he was, a royal grandson of King Saul entitled to live like royalty, he would have understood. By all rights, had Jonathan lived, Mephibosheth would have been heir to the throne. But he had lost sight of that and settled for less than his father intended for him.

In that same way, the devil convinces us that we are unworthy to know the King personally. Our circumstances have deceived us and blinded us to the truth of who we are—children of the King, and heirs of the kingdom.

The King's wish is to know us intimately

> *So the king said to him, "Where is he?" And Ziba said to the king, "Indeed he is in the house of Machir the son of Ammiel, in Lo Debar." Then King David sent and brought him out of the house of Machir the son of Ammiel, from Lo Debar. (2 Samuel 9:4-5)*

Just as King David sought out Mephibosheth, so the Lord Jesus has come to seek and to save lost humanity. The Holy Spirit is the Agent the Father uses to call us to Himself, like David used Ziba the servant, to seek out Mephibosheth. Mephibosheth came before the king, humbled himself as an unworthy person, and submitted himself as a servant. This should be the picture of any believer who comes to Jesus, who said, "If anyone will come after me, let him deny himself, take up his cross daily and follow me.' Mephibosheth considered himself unworthy to even be in the presence of the king. King David's response to him was the same as Jesus' is to us today:

> *And be kind to one another, tenderhearted, forgiving one another, even as God in Christ forgave you. (Ephesians 4:32)*

The picture could not be more graphic—the King is restoring the fallen to the position to which he was intended. He wished to know him intimately because he didn't come to just rescue someone who was down and out, but he wanted to build a relationship with him. In like manner, when Jesus came to this earth in human form to pay for our sin and to rescue us, He came to know us personally and for us to know Him.

> *I have come that they may have life, and that they may have it more abundantly. (John 10:10)*

This life was to consist of a fellowship with the King. David wanted Mephibosheth to become a part of his royal family in an intimate love relationship. In like manner, God desires that kind of relationship with us[10].

> *This is the message which we have heard from Him and declare to you, that God is light and in Him is no darkness at all. If we say that we have fellowship with Him, and walk in darkness, we lie and do not practice the truth. But if we walk in the light as He is in the light, we have fellowship with one another, and the blood of Jesus Christ His Son cleanses us from all sin. If we say that we have no sin, we deceive ourselves, and the truth is not in us. (1 John 1:5-8)*

Paul gives further explanation of this desired relationship in Romans 5:8-11. Jesus did not come to this earth just to pay for our sins, but that also He might live His life through us.

> *But God demonstrates His own love toward us, in that while we were sinners, Christ died for us. Much more then, having now been justified by His blood, we shall be saved from wrath through Him. For if when we were enemies we were reconciled to God through the death of His Son, much more, having been reconciled, we shall be saved by His life. And not only that, but we also rejoice in God through our Lord Jesus Christ, through whom we have now received the reconciliation. (Romans 5:8-11)*

Mephibosheth could not carry out a worthwhile life because of his crippled condition, so the king gave him servants to help. So we too are "saved by His life," the life of the Holy Spirit in us. David so much as told Mephibosheth, "I know you can't farm the land because of your condition. I know your limitations. But now you are a child of the king and what you can't do for yourself, I will do for you." You can't, I never said you could; I can, and I always said I would.

The Christian life is about allowing God the Holy Spirit to live His life in us. That life involves a surrender of our will to His, knowledge of His Word and what He wants to do through us. It involves knowing Him intimately.

The King's wish is to bless us abundantly

> *So David said to him, "Do not fear, for I will surely show you kindness for Jonathan your father's sake,*

and will restore to you all the land of Saul your grandfather; and you shall eat bread at my table continually." (2 Samuel 9:7)

This verse is what Paul meant when He wrote, "I can do all things through Christ who strengthens me[11]." In Adam, we lost the first estate of innocence. Crippled by the fall, we became sinners. But in Christ, we have been restored by a new birth and adopted into the King's family. His resources are now ours through the Holy Spirit. Our relationship of grace is not dependent on our being good or performing at a certain level.

This relationship of love honors a commitment made in eternity. "I don't understand it, no man is worthy of this!" Now you've got it. This is what grace is all about[12]. If salvation could have come as a result of our works, then Jesus would never have had to die for us. If Mephibosheth could have taken care of himself, then the king would not have had to honor his covenant with Jonathan.

OCCUPANTS OF THE KING'S DOMAIN

I don't know what these next verses mean to you, but the picture of our redemption is awesome. I wonder sometimes just how many Christians grasp the truth portrayed here.

Then Ziba said to the king, "According to all that my lord the King has commanded his servant, so will your servant do." "As for Mephibosheth," said the king, "he shall eat at my table like one of the king's sons." Mephibosheth had a young son whose name was Micha. And all who dwelt in

> *the house of Ziba were servants of Mephibosheth. So Mephibosheth dwelt in Jerusalem, for he ate continually at the king's table. And he was lame in both his feet. (2 Samuel 9:11-10:1)*

An unaltered position

Here we see the king giving Mephibosheth his inheritance; in essence the very inheritance that would have been his if Jonathan had inherited all that belonged to Saul. The position in the eleventh verse of 2 Samuel 9. Note the phrase: "Like one of the king's sons." David gave Mephibosheth a position equal to that of his own children.

The last verse reads: " . . . for he ate continually at the king's table." That means for the rest of his life, he was considered a part of the king's family. The position you and I have in salvation as God's children is the same kind of position. It has never been made clearer than Paul wrote in Ephesians 1:1-6:

> *And you He made alive, who were dead in trespasses and sins, in which you once walked according to the course of this world, according to the prince of the power of the air, the spirit who now works in the sons of disobedience, among whom also we all once conducted ourselves in the lusts of our flesh, fulfilling the desires of the flesh and of the mind, and were by nature children of wrath, just as the others. But God, who is rich in mercy, because of His great love with which He loved us, even when we were dead in trespasses, made us alive together, and made us sit together in the heavenly places in Christ Jesus.*

An unlimited portion

Paul further illustrates our position in Christ in Romans 8:15-17:

> *For you did not receive the spirit of bondage again to fear, but you received the Spirit of adoption by whom we cry "Abba, Father." The Spirit Himself bears witness with our spirit that we are children of God, and if children, then heirs—heirs of God and joint heirs with Christ, if indeed we suffer with Him, that we may also be glorified together.*

We are not guests, but heirs. The position is that of a family member because we have been adopted into the family of God. The Father looks at us as He looks at Jesus, as heirs and joint heirs.

This position is not only a position unaltered, but also a portion unlimited. Just as Mephibosheth was told that he would eat at the king's table always, so shall we be cared for by Him in the same way.

An unbelievable pardon

When Mephibosheth came to bow before the king, he expected to be dealt with like a fugitive. His father had long since been dead. Mephibosheth did not know about the agreement between Jonathan and David, so he fully expected to be treated as one of the king's enemies. But not so. He was restored to a position beyond his fondest expectations. Each of us who has experienced the grace of God has received an unbelievable pardon.

> *For if when we were enemies, we were reconciled to God through the death of His Son, much more, having been reconciled, we shall be saved by His life. And not only that, but we also rejoice in God through our reconciliation. (Romans 5:10-11)*

Let me ask you to use your sanctified imagination for just a minute. Imagine you are sitting at the dinner table of King David. It is a long table with numerous high-backed chairs. Imagine the long, white linen tablecloth draped over the table, a large candelabra in the center and food in abundance. If we listen, we can hear the King's family coming to dinner by the shuffle of feet as they walk down the hall to the dining room. One sounds different though, like someone is dragging his feet and walking with difficulty. They all enter the dining room and pull out the chairs to take their seats and we see that it is Mephibosheth who is crippled, whose steps were different. The King's children are all seated and the long white tablecloth drapes over the laps of all.

If we could be under the table, viewing the children from a worm's eye view, we would see many pairs of feet in their shoes. They all look pretty much the same except for one pair. They are worn on the sides instead of the soles; they are twisted and face in the wrong direction. But the king sits at the head of the table and looks down at all those at dinner. He doesn't see the feet under the table, just their faces, because the linen tablecloth covers all the feet.

> *Let us be glad and rejoice and give Him glory, for the marriage of the Lamb has come, and His wife has made herself ready." And to her it was granted to be arrayed in fine linen, clean and bright, for the*

fine linen is the righteous acts of the saints. Then he said to me, "Write: 'Blessed are those who are called to the marriage supper of the Lamb!'" And he said to me, 'These are the true sayings of God.'"
(Revelation 19:7-9)

"The fine linen is the righteousness of the saints." When Our King looks around the table at the Marriage of the Lamb, He will not see our twisted humanity, marred and mangled by sin. Our sins will be covered by His righteousness, and He will see us as He sees Jesus.

Beloved, now we are children of God; and it has not yet been revealed what we shall be, but we know that when He is revealed, we shall be like Him, for we shall see Him as He is. (1 John 3:2)

A story comes to us from Canada, at the end of World War II, when the Duke of Windsor made a Good Will Tour visiting various Veterans Hospitals. He went through the hospitals, room to room, shaking hands with the wounded, thanking them for their bravery and for serving their country.

He came to one ward with a "No Visitors—Keep Out" sign on the door. Curiosity got the better of him, and when nobody was looking, he slipped into the ward. It was a room with the most severely wounded veterans. The Duke found himself standing over a bed containing the torso of a man with no arms or legs. He also realized that the man could neither hear nor speak. He simply stared up into the eyes of the Duke with a hopeless loss of communication.

The Duke had the same sense of hopelessness. He could not shake the soldier's hand, for he had no hands. Nor could he speak to him with words of thanks, for the soldier could not hear. But with a gesture of grandeur, with tears pouring from his eyes, he reached into the bed, scooped up the body in his arms and brought the soldier to his bosom. He planted a kiss on the soldier's forehead and their tears mingled together as the Duke communicated his love and gratitude.

When Jesus came to Earth, He found us helpless in our sins. We could not understand God's love, and so He communicated that love to us by going to the cross to die in order to pay our sin debt. Like Mephibosheth, we were down and out. But because of Jesus, we have been scooped up into the presence of the King because of the noble gesture of the cross.

Look for the bridge of grace!

CHAPTER FOUR

THE PERFECT STORM

The year 2005 will long be remembered as "The Year of the Hurricanes." Katrina, Rita, and Wilma were the most memorable in a season so full of storms that those who name hurricanes exhausted our alphabet and moved to the Greek alphabet in search of new ones. The Gulf Coast from Texas to Florida was hammered and New Orleans flooded, bringing devastation and tragedy in a magnitude that the United States will never forget.

A few years ago, George Clooney starred in a movie entitled, "The Perfect Storm." You may remember the setting—a picturesque fishing village on the east coast. The fishermen were watching the weather reports on television, debating whether they should make their usual run with a major storm brewing. In one scene, two meteorologists were discussing the storm approaching from the southeast that would likely collide with an existing storm with record winds coming from the north. "You could live your whole life and never see a storm like this one . . . it may well be "the perfect storm."

The character played by Clooney and his shipmates calculated the risk and decided to go for it. They sailed into the hurricane-force winds and all the men were lost as the boat capsized in the storm. The "perfect storm" strangely enough was named "Hurricane Grace."

Life is full of storms—finances, health, relationships, loss of life, loss of jobs, divorce—all potentially devastating storms on the sea of life. Therefore, we need to know how we can turn our storms into "perfect storms." For the answer, we will look into Mark's gospel at Jesus and the disciples as they encountered a storm on the Sea of Galilee. If you remember, Jesus had left the seaside with his disciples rather abruptly. He was weary from ministry and lay down in the back of the boat after He instructed them to go to the other side of the sea.

Shortly after He fell asleep, a fierce wind came out of nowhere and threatened the boat and the lives of its passengers. The fearful disciples shouted to the sleeping Jesus: "Master, Master, don't you care if we perish?" He awoke, and then calmed the sea with the words, "Peace be still." Then He asked an amazing question: "Why are you so fearful? Where is your faith?" If we can answer those two questions correctly, we will find the secret to the "perfect storm."

DON'T LET THE CIRCUMSTANCES OVERWHELM YOU!

What can we learn from the overwhelmed disciples?

The first thing we can learn is that *we must look to Jesus and not at the storm*. In the narrative, the disciples were so concerned about perishing that they woke Jesus from His much-needed sleep. "Teacher, do you not care that we are perishing?" They had already drawn the conclusion that they were going to die and Jesus didn't care. If they had seen Jesus in the correct light, their attitudes would have been different.

Isn't this the case for many today in the midst of their storms? Many have a tendency to blame God as though He is asleep at the wheel or just doesn't care about them. Either view reveals an inadequate understanding of Jesus. Don't they realize that He is the Incarnate Son of God? Don't they realize that He is the One who created and controls the universe and nothing can happen to us without His permission? If the disciples' perspective of Jesus had been correct, their response to the danger would have been different. His probing question—"where is your faith?"—went straight to the problem. When our faith is in the boat or in our circumstances, we are in deep trouble. But if our faith is in Jesus, then we need not worry.

What can we learn from the overwhelming storm?

We can learn that *in the storm we can discover our source of peace.* Some years ago, I saw a painting that I shall never forget. It was a west coast seascape with a raging sea and dark clouds forming the background of a rainstorm on the ocean. The waves beat up against the jagged rocks and a tiny bird could be seen nestled in the cleft of one of the rocks. The little bird was safe in its shelter, and the title of the painting said it all: "Sheltered in the Midst of the Storm."

When we are sheltered in life's storm, *we can find out just how much Jesus cares for us.* Have you noticed that the things that get our attention the quickest are the things we really care about? My wife, Lynda, is a very sound sleeper. I believe someone could break into our house and carry off the furniture without waking her up. But when our children were small and one of them would cry out in the night, she heard them the instant they called. God wants us to wake Him up. It shows Him how much we depend on Him and it also gives Him the opportunity to show how much He cares for us. During the hurricanes on the Gulf coast, thousands of people experienced the love of God expressed through the benevolence of caring people.

In the storm, the disciples saw Jesus' caring in a way they might not have ever experienced otherwise. He became more than just the teacher; He became the caring Lord in their time of crisis.

The storms of life are also a good place *for God to get our attention.* It's amazing how many people come to a closer walk with the Lord as a result of a crisis in their lives. The Old Testament prophet, Jonah, is a good example. Jonah knew what God wanted from him, but he was not willing to go to Ninevah to preach to the pagans. In rebellion against God's will and the purpose of God for his life, he ran into a storm at sea. After three days in the belly of the fish, Jonah's attention was focused on God's will and he reconsidered his vocation in life! Sometimes it's easy to ignore God until we find ourselves in a storm with no way out and suddenly, He has our full attention.

Let us always remember that finding ourselves in a storm is *a good place to see God at work.* God can sleep through the things that keep us up at night. The worst storm we can encounter is no match for His grace. Without the storms, we'd never discover how God can meet every need we have. The storms can make us better or they can make us bitter—the choice is ours.

Wallace Hamilton, the greater preacher and author of another generation tells the story of a family experiencing a storm in the night that came blowing in with loud, crashing thunder and flashing lightning. The parents were worried that their little boy, an only child fast asleep upstairs, might awaken and be frightened. The father tiptoed upstairs and peeked into their son's room. Imagine his surprise to see the little fellow out of bed in front of the partially opened window, crying out, "Bang it again, God, bang it again!

DON'T LET YOUR DOUBTS UNDERMINE YOU

The words, "Master, don't you care that we perish," tell the whole story. *The disciples saw doubt, not deity.* It's so easy to be pessimistic rather than positive when things are going wrong. I have met some wonderful people who seem to always see the good in everything. They are the incurable optimists who just believe that things are going to work out. They aren't overlooking reality; they just have incredible hope. Storms are going to come our way and on many occasion, disaster is a reality. But it is more important to focus on the eternal perspective. We must not lose sight of the fact that God is in ultimate control of our lives and nothing can harm us without His permission. When hardship comes our way, we must look to Him to take us through it, knowing that there is a reason for it that we don't yet understand.

We must be reminded that Romans 8:28 is not in the Bible by accident. *"All things work together for the good for those who love God and are called to His purpose."* We might do well to ask the questions, "Am I called?" "Do I love God?" If the answers are "yes," then we must rest in the promise that He is at work no matter how painful the circumstances may be. An old hymn says, "We will understand it better by and by."

When my pastor friend, Buckner Fanning, had a tragedy in his family a few years ago, a lady in his church tried to comfort him by saying, "Pastor, one of these days you will look back on this and see how God was in it all." The next Sunday, Dr. Fanning preached a sermon entitled, "I'm Looking Forward to Looking Back." We all have those days when we think we cannot go on, but we must remember that in those times, Deity is at work in our circumstances.

I'm afraid we have to say that some people in the storm of life *see the gory and not the glory.* The first Christian martyr, Stephen, is a prime example. Instead of the gory, his own death by stoning, he saw the glory of God and Jesus standing at the right hand of God. He then prayed for his killers' forgiveness.

A number of years ago, we had a guest speaker in our church from Romania. Banished by Communist leader Checheskue, Joseph Tson sponsored an underground seminary for the study of Scriptures, and his books and tapes were widespread in Romania. He was imprisoned and commanded to release the names of all the other preachers in Romania. He refused because he knew they would be rounded up and killed. His persecutors beat him unmercifully, but day after day he refused to give them the names. One day, the beating was more than he could bear, and he cried out for mercy. The beating that day had spattered the walls with blood as his head was repeatedly bashed against the wall.

When he was returned to his cell, he realized that it was Good Friday. Dr. Tson said, "I realized that Jesus had also suffered, laid down His life and gone to the cross for me over 2000 years ago on that very same day. I got down on my knees and asked God to forgive me for being such a coward. The next day he was summoned once again for his daily punishment. But before his captors began the interrogation, Tson said, 'I have an apology to make to you. I want you to forgive me for my behavior yesterday. When I got back to my cell, I realized that 2000 years ago, on this same day, my Lord died for me that I might be saved. The least I can do is to be willing to do the same for Him.

"Your weapon is killing, but mine is dying. Go ahead and kill me, but when you do, my name will be greater than ever. My sermons and my books will take on new meaning and be read even more because I will have laid down my life for Christ." His accusers realized that he spoke the truth. So they released him from prison and exiled him from Romania.

He came to America to tell his story, but has returned to Romania and, to my knowledge, continues to preach and tell his story all over the world. He, too, looked past the gory and saw God's glory.

WE MUST LET HIS POWER OVERCOME US

> *But He said to them, "Why are you so fearful? How is it that you have no faith?" And they feared exceedingly, and said to one another, "Who can this be, that even the wind and the sea obey Him!" (Mark 4:40-41)*

The disciples were more *overcome by the calm than by the storm.* The Greek word used here for "fear" is a different word than the one used earlier in the passage. This one is a word for reverence and awe: "To terrify."[1] This is the same word used when the angels spoke to Joseph in Matthew 1:18. Suddenly, the disciples were aware that they were in the presence of divine power and personality. We, too, are drawn closer to the Lord Jesus in our storms than we are in ordinary circumstances. Speak to almost anyone who has been there, and they can testify of the awesome presence of God that allowed them to know Him significantly better. Though we would not choose to go through them again, these are the experiences we value above all others.

I remember a particular story from one person whose experience left him *overcome with a reverence at His presence*. This individual had a heart attack and while in surgery, had an "out of body" experience. He could literally see himself lying unconscious on the operating table as doctors feverishly worked to keep him alive. Up until this time, he had not been a believer in Christ. The week after he was released from the hospital, he came to church, walked down the aisle at the close of the service and made a profession of faith. He remains a faithful servant of Christ until this day.

When we *fear (reverence) Jesus more than anything else*, we enter into the experience of a perfect storm. When we rest in Him and are overcome by His presence, we can have a perfect storm. When we come to the place of knowing that He is ours and we are His, we can let the storms come and go because we have learned to go through them with Him for He is our only hope.

I will never forget a lesson I learned from my Dad when I was a small boy about ten years of age. Our family often went on camping trips to a large lake in Southeast Arkansas where my Dad would fish. I didn't care a thing about fishing, but I did like to run the motorboat. It was a small three-and-a-half horsepower motor and not too powerful for a ten year old to operate. The lake was large, about a mile wide and fifteen miles long. One afternoon, just before supper, I was out in the boat in the middle of the lake when a windstorm came up. The white-capped waves were crashing over the sides of the boat and filling the boat with water. I could hear my father calling instructions from the shore. Between his gestures and voice, I managed to understand: "Son, keep the nose into the waves, give her full throttle, and keep your eyes on me."

I made it back to camp and into the welcoming arms of Mom and Dad. That lesson has become a motto in my life. When you are in the storm, whatever it may be, *keep your nose into the waves, give her full throttle, and keep your eyes on the Father.*" I promise He will bring you through every time.

Keep your eyes on the Bridge Builder!

CHAPTER FIVE

THE DANGER OF BELIEVING A LIE

There is great danger in believing a lie.

I remember years ago reading a story in Readers Digest about a Presbyterian minister in a small Georgia town who was counseling a woman in his study at his home. The woman made advances toward him much like Potipher's wife did to Joseph. The minister kindly refused her. The woman, who felt rejected and was bent on getting even with the minister, left his house, went out on the front porch, ripped her dress and began to scream. The neighbors heard her and came to see what the commotion was about. She accused the minister of trying to seduce her. The minister lost his church and had to leave the ministry. Twenty-five years later, when the woman lay sick and dying with cancer, she wanted to make her peace with God. She called for the elders of the church and confessed her lie about the pastor whose career she had ruined.

The Bible identifies the devil as the father of lies. There are several different kinds of lies, and ever since the Garden of Eden, Satan has used all of them to deceive mankind. First, there is the outright lie. Second, there is the silent lie, which is used to lead people to believe circumstantial evidence. Third, a lie is perpetrated when evidence is misrepresented so that people draw the wrong conclusion. The fourth kind of lie is an innuendo or insinuation.

Genesis 37:31-36 breaks into the middle of two generations of biblical history concerning the lives of Jacob and his son Joseph. Certain events in their lives illustrate the biblical truth of the danger of believing a lie.

LIES BLUR THE REALITIES OF OUR DREAMS

Jacob was known as a trickster. He had stolen the birthright of his twin brother, Esau, who was the firstborn of the two. Jacob had deceived their father (Isaac) into giving him Esau's special blessing. In Genesis 28, Jacob was fleeing from his homeland because of Esau's wrath. In addition, Jacob's parents did not want him to take a wife from among the women living around them, so Isaac sent him to his uncle's house to find a wife.

The first night of the fugitive's flight was spent on a rock, and in Genesis 28:12-15 we read, *"Then he dreamed, and behold, a ladder was set up on the earth, and its top reached to heaven; and there the angels of God were ascending and descending on it. And behold, the Lord stood above it and said: "I am the Lord God of Abraham your father and the God of Isaac; the land on which you lie I will give to you and your descendants. Also your descendants shall be as the dust of the earth; you shall spread abroad to the west and east, to the north and the south; and in you and in your seed all the families of the earth shall be blessed. Behold, I am with you and will keep you wherever you go, and will bring you back to this land; for I will not leave you until I have done what I have spoken to you."*

Jacob awoke from his sleep and said, *"'Surely the Lord is in this place, and I did not know it.' And he was afraid and said, 'How awesome is this place!' . . ."* (Genesis 28:16-17). As a boy, Jacob had heard the stories about God and his father, Isaac, and his grandfather, Abraham. Now he had met God face to face! In a marvelous manner, God revealed that He had bridged the gap between heaven and earth (the ladder) and made it possible for sinful man to be in His holy presence.

Even more than that, God spoke to Jacob and gave him three promises: for provision—*"the land on which you lie I will give to you and your descendants;"* for prosperity—*"your descendants shall be as the dust of the earth . . . and in your seed all the families of the earth shall be blessed;"* and for protection—*"I am with you and will keep you wherever you go . . . . I will not leave you until I have done what I have spoken to you."*

This dream gave Jacob an overwhelming awareness of the presence of God—*"How awesome is this place!"* he exclaimed, *"This is none other than the house of God, and this is the gate of heaven!"* (Genesis 28:17). He was so awed by this that he made a vow: *"If God will be with me . . . so that I come back to my father's house in peace, then the Lord shall be my God. And this stone which I have set as a pillar shall be God's house, and of all that You give me I will surely give a tenth to You"* (Genesis 28:20-22).

Surely this great dream, this encounter with Almighty God, energized Jacob to live the rest of his live victoriously. But in our text passage we find that Joseph's older brothers have deceived Jacob into thinking Joseph was dead, and verses 34-35 tell us, *"Then Jacob tore his clothes, put sackcloth on his waist, and mourned for his son many days . . . he refused to be comforted, and he said, 'For I shall go down into the grave to my son in mourning.'"* Jacob forgot his dream, forgot the promises God made him, forgot the awesomeness of God's presence in his life. The reality of his great experience was blurred when be believed the lies of his sons.

LIES ROB US OF
THE VITALITY OF OUR VICTORIES

Jacob's grief over the supposed death of his son also robbed him of the vitality of a great victory he had previously experienced. In Genesis 32, we find the account in which, as a younger man, he wrestled with God.

This event occurred as Jacob was getting ready to confront his brother Esau. Esau was coming to meet Jacob and was bringing four hundred men with him. Jacob did not know whether or not Esau was still angry with him, and he was very afraid. He sent messengers ahead of him with presents for Esau, hoping to pacify him.

Meanwhile, Jacob prayed for God to deliver him. In Genesis 32:24-28 we read, *"Then Jacob was left alone; and a Man wrestled with him until the breaking of day. Now when He saw that He did not prevail against Him, He touched the socket of his hip; and the socket of Jacob's hip was out of joint as He wrestled with him. And He said 'Let Me go, for the day breaks.' But he said, 'I will not let You go You bless me!; . . . .*

And He said, 'Your name shall no longer be called Jacob, but Israel [Prince with God]; for you have struggled with God and with men, and have prevailed.'" What a glorious victory for Jacob!

For over twenty years, Jacob had been operating in the flesh, living in fear of the brother he had tricked. For him, this was a victory over the flesh, and it is significant that he was made lame by this battle. He held onto the Angel of the Lord until he was victorious, but in the process he was broken when the Angel put his hip out of joint.

The same thing has to happen to any Christian who has been operating in his own strength. He has been living on pride and must be broken before God can use him. After Jacob wrestled with the Angel, he was successfully reconciled with his brother—but he bore a limp until the day he died.

Surely a victory like this could have carried him through the rest of his life! But it didn't. Instead of facing his tragedy in the light of his past dreams and victories, be believed a lie and he was robbed of his vitality.

LIES ROB US OF THE POTENTIAL FOR THE PRESENT

In Genesis 39-45, we find that Joseph was not dead, but that he had been sold into slavery and ended up in Egypt. There, his master's wife lied about him and he was put in prison. In prison, God gave Joseph the interpretation of the dreams of two men who had worked in the household of Pharoah, the ruler of Egypt. One man died; the other returned to his job. When Pharoah had a disturbing dream that he wanted interpreted, the chief butler remembered Joseph and told Pharoah about him. Joseph was brought out of prison, and God gave him the interpretation of Pharoah's dream. As a result, Pharoah made Joseph his governor, second in power only to himself.

While all of this was happening to Joseph, Jacob was back in Israel, still mourning Joseph as dead. He had completely lost sight of God's promises to him. He was not concerned with the present or the future. All he wanted was to die and be with his son. But all along, God was preparing Joseph in Egypt to take care of his father for the coming famine and fulfill God's promises to Jacob: to take care of him, multiply his descendants, and bring him back to the land he had left behind.

When the famine came upon the land, Jacob sent his sons to Egypt, Joseph recognized them, but they did not recognize him. Having not seen them for so many years and not knowing what they were like, he tested them. When he found out that they were truly sorry for what they had done to him, he revealed who he was and sent them back to get his father and all of their families and possessions and come to live in Egypt where he could take care of them. Jacob's reaction to the news is found in Genesis 45:26-28: " . . . . *Jacob's heart stood still, because he did not believe them. But when they told him all the words which Joseph had said . . . the spirit of Jacob their father revived. Then Israel said, 'It is enough. Joseph my son is still alive. I will go and see him before I die.'"*

Believing a lie had blurred the reality of Jacob's dreams and robbed him of the vitality of his victories and his potential. Notice that when the lie was exposed and he was revived, the Scripture refers to him in the next instance as Israel [Prince with God], not Jacob [Supplanter]. The message here for us is that when we dare to believe a lie, it steals away the potential for the present moment. We forget that the Lord has saved us for a purpose and promised to take care of us. We take our eyes off of His sovereignty and fall into unnecessary grief—wasting time and resources that God could be using for our good. That is the danger of believing a lie!

> ***The bridge of forgiveness takes you***
> ***over the bitter waters of resentment.***

CHAPTER SIX

BLESSINGS UNLIMITED

The word "blessing" seems to be a favorite of believers everywhere—in prayers, in songs, and in everyday conversation. Several years ago, one of the deacons in my church closed every prayer with these words: "Lord, suit a blessing to each of us, Amen." And most of us remember the old hymns about "Showers of Blessings," and "Make Me a Blessing." After I've preached a sermon, people have said to me, "Preacher, you have been a blessing to me."

I have often wondered just what that word really means. When I turn to Webster, I find that it has more than one definition, but chiefly: "To invoke divine care for."[1] But my favorite is the definition a friend gave in a sermon: "*A blessing is the sovereign act of God upon someone or something that causes it to supernaturally produce more than would be naturally possible.*"

This definition more nearly describes the passage of Scripture in Matthew 14:13-21 that tells about the miracle of Jesus feeding the five thousand. Jesus had been preaching in the area and had performed several miracles and people were following after him for days. The disciples pointed out to Him that the crowds were growing weak with hunger. Jesus answered, tongue in cheek, "you feed them then." They answered, "We have only five loaves and two fish." Jesus then asked for the fish and the loaves and told the people to sit down on the grassy area.

Then Jesus did a strange thing. The scripture says, "Looking to heaven, He blessed and broke and gave the loaves to His disciples and the disciples distributed the food to the multitude." This was indeed a sovereign act of God upon five loaves and two fish to supernaturally produce more than naturally possible. With this definition in mind, I want you to consider four thoughts.

GOD'S BLESSINGS ARE NOT LIMITED BY THE SIZE OF OUR NEED

The "too much" attitude

Some people have the attitude that there are just some things that are too much for which to ask God. They conclude that it is beyond His reach or that He would not be able to handle the enormity of their request. That was the unspoken attitude of the disciples:

> *When it was evening, His disciples came to Him saying, "This is a deserted place, and the hour is already late. Send the multitudes away, that they may go into the*

> *villages and buy themselves food." But Jesus said to them, "They do not need to go away. You give them something to eat." And they said to Him, "We have here only five loaves and two fish." (Matthew 14:15-17)*

The disciples had concluded that the need was greater than their ability to meet, and even though Jesus had done unbelievable things in their presence, they obviously did not count Him in on the solution to the problem. Their attitude was, "this is too much, even for Jesus."

How many times have we had that same attitude? How many times have we looked everywhere for a solution to the problem before bringing it to God? He has been waiting for such a need to arise in order to bless us, but we hesitate to call on Him. However, it is when we call that we find He is able to meet our every need.

A great Old Testament story from the lives of Abraham and Sarah illustrates this attitude. Because Sarah had been unable to conceive, Abraham asked God to let his servant become the heir, but God said, "No, I will give you an heir from your own seed." Years went by and Abraham grew tired of waiting; besides, Sarah had another plan. She suggested that Abraham have a child with Hagar, her servant. He agreed, and Ishmael was born.

Then God told them that Plan B was unacceptable—they would have a child of their own. Sure enough, Sarah conceived and Isaac was born. They named him Isaac, because Isaac means "laughter" and Sarah had laughed when God told her she would become a mother at 90+ years. God had waited until it was humanly impossible for Abraham and Sarah to bear a child so that He could bless them with a sovereign act of God that supernaturally produced more than was humanly possible.

We need to remember to go to God first with our needs when things seem impossible—"is there anything too hard for God"?

The "too little" attitude

A second attitude exists that might suggest our resources are too limited to solve our problem. The disciples had both attitudes. They thought the problem was "too big," and then they thought the two fish and five loaves were "too little." Jesus knew all along what they thought and what they would learn from this testing. Until we bring our "too little" to Jesus, we will never have "too much."

GOD'S BLESSINGS ARE NOT LIMITED BY THE CAUSE OF OUR NEED

Sometimes our need arises from neglect

The multitudes that followed Jesus were so caught up in the excitement of hearing Him speak that they had not made adequate preparation. They ended up far from their homes, exhausted and hungry.

We have all gotten ourselves into situations that could have been avoided if we'd made adequate preparations or given forethought to where we could end up. We even rationalize our predicament, saying, "I got myself into this mess, so it's up to me to get myself out." Then we remember: "God helps those who help themselves!" But God didn't say that, Benjamin

Franklin did! The truth is that God helps those who cannot help themselves.

Another example of this truth is when Peter saw Jesus walking on the water and called out, "Master, bid me come to you." Jesus said, "Come on." Then, miraculously, Peter walked on water, too; that is, until he started looking around at the wind and the waves. Peter panicked, "and, beginning to sink, cried out, "Lord, save me!" (Matthew 14:30)

That should tell us something about Jesus and ourselves. First, if you never dare to do anything adventurous for the Lord, you can stay in the boat all your life. Second, you can do some unbelievable things if you keep your eyes on Jesus. Third, fear is a very defeating factor in all our lives. Peter didn't begin to sink until he took his eyes off the Savior and became fearful of the winds and the waves.

Sometimes our need arises from fear

Fear often keeps us from attempting anything great for God. We talk ourselves out of grand ideas and adventures before we even attempt them because we fear failure. Let's give Simon Peter his due. He is the only man besides the Lord to walk on water. At least he was not afraid to try.

The thought processes that begin with . . . "God could never bless me because . . ." "I'm too bad" . . . "I'm too small" . . . I'm not smart enough" . . . are straight out of the pit. God has a strange way of blessing those who show up with courage and report for duty. Remember David and Goliath? Remember little Samuel? Remember Moses? Remember Gideon? None of them were perfect by a long shot, but they were willing to try. And the sovereign act of God upon their lives supernaturally produced what was naturally impossible.

GOD'S BLESSINGS ARE NOT LIMITED TO VISIBLE RESOURCES AT HAND

The disciples looked around, couldn't see anything that would indicate resources to feed five thousand people, and assumed the obvious. But with God, the obvious is not always so obvious.

Some years ago, I was the pastor of a small church in Phoenix, Arizona. I had gone to the church with the understanding that we would relocate the church on a larger portion of property. Though we were a small congregation, the three wealthiest men in Arizona Baptist Life were members of the church. I accepted the call, counting on the strength of these men and their wealth. Little did I know that in the first year of my ministry, two of the men would move to California and the third would die. This reduced me to my last resort . . . God. I should have started with Him, of course, and so I learned a real lesson in faith. In less than three years, we relocated the church from a four-acre location to one with 15 acres. Though none of the money came from the obvious visible sources, we were able to build new buildings that doubled the size of the worship space.

The disciples learned that day how Jesus could feed five thousand people with no visible resources at hand. "He took the fish and the loaves and looking to heaven, He blessed and broke and gave to His disciples." Here, my friends, are "blessings unlimited." When there seemed to be no other way to feed the hungry multitude, Jesus asked the Father for

His special involvement in the situation. This is the kind of thing God loves to do for His children.

God loves for us to get into ministry situations that demand our faith. He loves being God, able to rescue, able to save, able to solve every problem. "Without faith it is impossible to please God," (Hebrews 11:6).

GOD'S BLESSINGS ARE UNLEASHED BY FAITH

The Bible is very clear about how to have faith. In Romans 1:17, we are told that "the just are to live by faith." It is through faith that we were saved and it is by faith that we are to live. Next, we need to understand the difference between having faith and just hoping hard. What is the difference? Romans 10:17 answers this by saying, "Faith comes by hearing and hearing by (through) the word of God."

The Greek word used here for "word" is *rhema*, not the more familiar word *logos*. Rhema means, in this case, "a word spoken to us by the Holy Spirit." When the logos, (written word), is spoken to us by the Spirit, it becomes the rhema of God upon which we may act in faith.

For instance, a person is listening to a sermon and hears the scripture, " . . . for God so loved the world that He gave His only begotten Son that whosoever believes on Him shall not perish, but have everlasting life." He's heard the logos, the written word. But suddenly, the Holy Spirit speaks that Scripture to his heart and he realizes that word is about him, and he receives a rhema from the Holy Spirit.

"It is impossible to please God without faith. He who comes to God must believe that He is and that He is a rewarder of those that seek Him" (Hebrews 11:6). "As you therefore have received Christ Jesus the Lord walk ye in Him," (Colossians 2:6). We received Him by faith and we walk in Him by receiving His word and acting upon His word. When Christians get hold of that truth, they begin to see God turn the impossible into the possible. His blessings are unlimited!

Some years ago I had an experience with our youngest son, Jeff, when he was about eight years old. About a month before Christmas, I met Jeff coming up the sidewalk one crisp, fall afternoon. He had a twinkle in his eyes as he met me in front of our house.

"Daddy, I know what I want Santa to bring me this Christmas."

"What's that son?"

"A bicycle," he replied.

Those words took me back to the time when I was the same age as Jeff. My first bike cost twenty-six dollars. I knew inflation had changed things, but I had no idea what bikes cost.

"Sure son," I answered. "I think Santa can handle that."

He went upstairs and I went into the kitchen where Lynda was. I told her what had just happened and she said, "I hope you didn't tell him that he could have that bicycle for Christmas. We have three other children and the bike he wants costs over $200." After some diligent budget negotiations, we agreed that he would get the bike, and Lynda swore me to secrecy.

A couple of weeks went by and Christmas was getting closer. One day, I met Jeff coming in the front door with a sad look on his face. When I asked what was wrong, he said, "I've been down to the bike shop and all the bicycles have "Sold" signs on them. I could not tell him that one was his, so I said,

Build a Bridge . . . and Get Over It! | 71

'Son, you'd better not count on a bike this Christmas." Days came and went and the cloud over his head remained.

Lynda is a stickler for having Christmas around the tree on Christmas day. But this particular year, because Christmas was on a Sunday, we persuaded her to open presents on Christmas Eve. On Christmas Eve morning, Jeff's friend Mike came riding down the street on his brand new bicycle, just like the one Jeff wanted. Jeff grew even more depressed. After dinner, we sent the kids upstairs while we put the presents under the tree.

Because Jeff's bicycle wouldn't fit under the tree, we put it across the hallway in our bedroom with the front wheel just sticking out so that he would eventually see it.

The kids came downstairs and rushed to the tree, but there were no presents there for Jeff. He began to look around, and then he saw it! When he spied the glitter of the spokes across the hall, he jumped straight up in the air. When he hit the floor, I fully expected him to run to that bicycle, hop on, and disappear out the front door. But he surprised me! He jumped into my arms, wrapped his arms around my neck and kissed me, and then he went to his mother, his grandparents, his sisters and even his brother. "Thank you, thank you," he repeated over and over to everyone in the room.

I couldn't stand it any longer. I walked across the room to the bike, pulled it to the door, opened the door, grabbed Jeff and shoved him out the door onto the sidewalk. The streetlights were beginning to come on as Lynda and I watched our eight-year-old ride down to Mike's to show his bike to his best friend.

I said, 'Honey, there is a sermon in this," and she gave me that "Here we go again" look. I said, "Who would have thought that Jeff would thank us first instead of rushing to the bicycle?" That's what our Father wants—for us to thank Him and love Him, the Blesser, more than we love the blessings. He's made the provisions to pour out His unlimited blessings on His children, "It is the Father's desire to give His children the Kingdom."

Thirty years later, that little boy has four children of his own. He rides a bicycle 30 to 100 miles a week and is the pastor of one of the fastest growing churches in our city. He is a blessing—A sovereign act of God upon someone or something causing it to supernaturally produce more than is naturally possible. The Father wants to bless you! Just love Him, put your arms around Him and thank Him and just watch what happens!

> ***The longest bridge of all is the bridge of faith;***
> ***but remember, it spans the distance between***
> ***earth's tragedies and Heaven's glory!***

CHAPTER SEVEN

PUT YOUR HOUSE IN ORDER

Some years ago, after I had bypass surgery, my doctor said to me, "I would really like to hear you preach for the next couple of weeks, because it's really going to be different for you."

I said, "What do you mean?"

He replied, "Well, you see, when people undergo anesthetic it usually lingers for several weeks after the surgery. Your reflexes are slow and you may have a tendency to go to sleep."

I laughed. "Don't worry about that! People do that all the time in my sermons! I guess it would be all right if I did that, too."

He smiled patiently and said, "You might even become emotional at times because you're recuperating, and it's more drastic than you may realize."

Well, I'm not sure about any of that. First of all, I have never had any emotions that I could not deal with (other than emotions of deep joy and of a great sense of the Lord's presence), but I want to share some things with you because of what this experience has meant to me, and, for what it's worth, to pass it onto some of you who are presently in the very situation that I found myself in.

Before my surgery, I don't suppose that I had ever really taken stock of my own life by asking, "What if I die?" While this was not my first experience with surgery, it was the first time to have anything this extensive; it was my first time to realize that I could die in the process.

I want to address that thought through the lens of one verse of scripture. In 2 Samuel 17:23, we find a character named Ahithophel. The scripture says that he **"set his house in order,"** and then went and hanged himself. We also find those very same words—**"set your house in order"**—in II Kings 20:1. This time it is spoken of Hezekiah, the king, who was mortally ill. Isaiah came to him and said, "Hezekiah, **set your house in order**, for you are going to die." The difference between Hezekiah and Ahithophel is that Hezekiah turned his face toward the Lord and began to pray, and God gave him fifteen additional years.

General Douglas McArthur once said, "A man is not prepared to live until he is prepared to die." These days, there are two rather curious ideas that exist in the minds of young people. First, young people think that they are the only folks who were ever young. Secondly, they think they are going to be young forever. I want to tell you there are not two thoughts further from the truth. First of all, you are not the only person who was ever young, and secondly, you better pray that you don't always stay young, because the only way to stay young forever is to die before you grow old!

Another great fallacy is that one has to be old to die. While I was in the hospital, a 24-year-old man died of a heart attack, and a six-year-old boy lay beside me in a coma. As far as I know, he is still in a coma. Death is not just for the old to think about. We need to think in terms of setting our house in order.

I want to ask you three questions:

WHY DOES A PERSON PUT HIS HOUSE IN ORDER?

Let me present the whole story of who Ahithophel was in a nutshell. Ahithophel was the counselor in Israel to David and later to Absalom. The scripture says, *"And the counsel of Ahithophel, which he counseled in those days, was as if a man had inquired of the oracle of God: so was all the counsel of Ahithophel both with David and with Absalom."* (2 Samuel 16:23) In other words, his counsel to the king was tantamount to having a word from God. When Ahithophel spoke counsel, they said, "That's law, we'll do it." So it was that David had carried Ahithophel along with him for a long, long time and most likely had known him from his very youth. When we read the scripture over in the Psalms we find David writing about a person, *"Yea, mine own familiar friend, in whom I trusted, which did eat of my bread, hath lifted up his heel against me"* (Psalm 41.9). In Psalm 55:12 we read, *"For it was not an enemy that reproached me; then I could have borne it: neither was it he that did magnify himself against me; then I would have hid myself from him; but it was thou, a man mine equal, my guide, and mine acquaintance. We took sweet counsel together, and walked unto the house of God in company."* You see, Ahithophel had been the counsel to David up until Absalom had begun to fight against David, and then Ahithophel changed sides. He was in a conspiracy against David. He said to Absalom, "Let me give you this counsel how David may be taken." Well, David prayed to the Lord that his counsel would be thwarted, and God raised up another man by the name of Hushai. Hushai's counsel, seemingly for the first time, was taken over against the counsel of Ahithophel. When Ahithophel found that his counsel was no longer taken by David, he couldn't stand it. So he went home, set his house in order, and then went out and hanged himself.

Because He Gets Serious About Dying

Why does a man ever set his house in order? First of all, he does it because he gets serious about dying.

In the days prior to my bypass surgery, I started to get serious about dying for the first time in my life. However, the problem is that death is not a popular subject to discuss with people. I found that when I got serious about dying, nobody wanted to talk to me about it. I had some things I wanted to say to Lynda. In the event I did die, I wanted to make sure that those things were said. She never wanted to talk about it! She refused to listen. Finally one night I just said to her, "Now listen, I've got some things that I'm going to tell you. Whether you want to hear them or not, I need to talk to you about it." She finally listened, but no one else wanted any part of such a conversation. I'd say something to my mother, or I'd say something to my kids, and they'd say, "Don't think about that, you're going to be all right." I knew that there were plenty of people who thought they were "going to be all right" and didn't make it. I was serious about dying, and I was determined to put my house in order.

On December 26, 1962, I stood on a bridge in a little town in Arkansas shooting turtles off of the bridge with my father. I liked the gun that he was shooting and I remarked, "Dad, why don't you sell me that gun? I know you horse traded a guy out of it, you don't have much money in it, and I want to buy it." I was in my last year of seminary at the time. He said to me, "No, son, I put this gun in my will for you because this is probably the last Christmas that we're going to have together." I said, "Don't give me that stuff; I don't want to hear about that. I don't believe that. You're going to live to be an old man." I went back to Seminary on the 27th of December, and he died less than four months later, on April 2nd. That day on the bridge was the last day that I saw him alive. He knew something. He was preparing to die. He had set his house in order.

Now, the act of setting your house in order doesn't necessarily result in someone dying. For example, one day I came home from work and called out for Lynda as usual, "Yoo-hoo, anybody home?" Nobody answered. The boys were gone. I wandered through the house looking for Lynda, and on my way, walked by the fireplace. There was a chair pulled up in front of the fireplace, Lynda's Bible was open, and there was a piece of paper in it. Nobody was around and the house was still. My curiosity got the best of me, and I picked up the piece of paper. At the top, in Lynda's handwriting, it read, "My Funeral Arrangements."

I thought, "My, what's happened?" I began to read it. It was an order of service for her funeral! It contained a detailed outline of who she wanted to pray, who she wanted to sing, who she wanted to preach the funeral, how she wanted it to be, and then it just trailed off and ended abruptly. I started going through the house, a little concerned now, calling, "Lynda, honey, where are you? Where are you?" No answer. I picked up the phone and called three or four neighbors. "Have you seen my wife?" I asked a bit frantically. "No, I haven't seen her anywhere," they would answer. Somebody said they had seen her early that morning, but as far as anyone knew, she was nowhere to be found!

I'm telling you what, I began to look under the beds . . . I began to look everywhere. I figured that maybe she got depressed and went out and ended it all. I hadn't realized it was so bad! My mind raced wildly as it sorted through every possible scenario. I was starting to panic!

It wasn't long before I heard the car drive up and she walked in the back door. I was sitting there in shock, holding the piece of paper, and I said, "Where have you been?" She said, "What do you mean?" I said, "Well, what's this?" I showed her the paper. (I'll tell you what really upset me: she had listed Dr. Webb as the one who would preach at her funeral! She loved Dr. Webb, and she loved to hear him pray, and she had *him* down there on that paper!) I said, "I sure hope you're going to be here long, long after he's gone, because he's much older than you!" I thought that this funeral was going to be something immediate. She said, "No—oh that!" I said, "Now what would you think if you came home and found your husband's funeral arrangements laid out and nobody home? What would you think? I'll tell you what you'd think. You'd think somebody was planning on dying!" She laughed and said, "You know, I had a dream last night. It was such a beautiful dream!" She shared with me the dream that she had—her funeral in detail!—and she said, "I wanted to write it down before I forgot it." This happened a long time ago, and thank the Lord she is still with us, but she made some plans and wrote down some things while they were fresh in her memory because she was thinking about dying.

When I went for my bypass surgery, they didn't even want to talk to me about dying in the hospital. Just before I went into surgery, the nurse came in and handed me a piece of paper and said, "We need you to sign right down here before we can do the surgery."

I said, "All right," and began to sign.

She said, "Don't you want to read it first?"

I said, "I trust you."

She frowned at me and said, "I suggest you read it first."

It was two pages long, and I started reading it. The last paragraph read, *"I understand that this may result in heart attack or even death."*

I said, "Wait a minute, I came in here to get well! What is this?"

"Oh, it's just a matter of formality. We put that everywhere." She didn't want to talk about it.

I asked, "Well, what's it on there for if we can't talk about it?"

I want to tell you something, folks: if your husband or wife or child is getting ready to undergo serious surgery, let them talk about it, because nobody ever has the assurance that they are going to return. When man thinks about dying, man thinks about getting his house in order, and that is a rightful thing. Unless Jesus comes back, one of these days I am going to die. You're going to die. Just because you don't want to talk about it or think about it doesn't mean that it won't happen. You had better set your house in order. Just because you set your house in order doesn't mean it's going to take place right away, but unless Jesus comes and raptures you out of this world, eventually you are going to die. That's part of setting you house in order. People set their house in order—why? **Because they are thinking seriously about death.** Young people, you need to think about it. Every year teenagers are buried. Every year little white caskets are brought down the aisle with children who have died and gone on, and whether you want to think about it or not is not important. It's the fact that death is as evident as life.

Because He Get Serious About Living

The second reason a person gets his house in order is because he gets serious about living. One day before my surgery, I was reading the scripture written by Paul in Philippians 1:21 which says, *"For me to live is Christ, but to die is gain."* I thought, "You know, Lord, I'm saved, I've got the victory. I've got the peace. Dying is no problem now. I've got it settled, and if You want to take me home, so be it. My problem will come if I live another thirty years. My potential problem is that I probably don't have enough money to retire in light of inflation these days. I'm probably not going to be able to be all that I need to be." The part in that verse that really bothered me is *"For me to live is Christ."* Was I willing to take the things out of my life that were keeping that from being so? Was I willing to say to the Lord Jesus Christ, "I am willing to be all that you want me to be for the next thirty years if perchance I do live?" It is much harder to live for Him than it is to die for Him. It's harder to say, as Paul said, *"For me to live is Christ."*

Ask yourself this question: what is it in my life that needs to be set in order—not because I may die, but because I may live? Some have marriages that are on the rocks. Some have personal habits that are unbecoming to Jesus. In these situations, you are not living as unto Christ; you are living as unto yourself. And Paul says, *"For me to **live** is Christ."* In other words, let Him through my life; if I die, that's gain.

As I pondered these things, I began to realize that, just as there was one tiny thing in my physical heart that was keeping me from being physically fit, there could also be enough sin in my life as the pastor of my church that could keep the church from being physically fit. If you think about it, in many ways the pastor is the heart of the church. Jesus is the head, but He moves through the heart—the pastor. Was I willing to have the kind of "bypass" necessary in my spiritual life in order to be what I need to be, so that I could say, "Lord, I'm not only serious about dying, but I'm serious about living . . . serious enough to get my house in order. I want to be all that you want me to be?" A lot of people today need to set their house in order so that they can be serious about living as unto the Lord rather than as unto yourself.

WHEN DOES A PERSON GET HIS HOUSE IN ORDER?

When does a man come to the place that he decides that he is going to set his house in order? Ahithophel did it in a particular time in his life: when he finally came to see the futility of his own life. He saw the frailty, the sinfulness, the shamefulness of it—to the point that he could not face life himself. Likewise, men and women begin to set things in order when they see the frailty and the futility of their own flesh. Ahithophel didn't set his house in order the way he ought to have. He was a man who offered sacrifice, as we are told in 2 Samuel 15:12, and he was a man who had some insight into God and at one time had spoken as though he had the oracles of God. However, the Bible tells us in 2 Samuel 17:23 that " . . . *they no longer took his counsel.*" When he saw his frailty, when he saw his finiteness and his sinfulness, when he saw all that he could not be, when his popularity failed him, when the frailty of his flesh manifest itself, he decided, "I'll get my house in order because it's not worth living."

Those are the same things that ought to happen to you. You will never set your house in order until you stand before the King—not king David, but King Jesus—and look at yourself in the light of the King and say, "I don't know it all." Ahithophel finally had to come to the realization he didn't know it all. I've got news for you: I don't know it all; neither do you. It's when we come to the realization that we do not have all of the answers and that we, in our flesh, are frail and fleeting that we must come to the realization that something has to be done.

Now, good, bad, or indifferent, Ahithophel did not handle his problem correctly. I think that King Hezekiah did. King Hezekiah turned his face toward the Lord. He began to pray to God, and God extended his life. He looked to the Lord and said, "Lord, I am setting my house in order, but first of all, I want you to know . . . ," and he pleaded with God, and God extended his life. You see, beloved, God is the giver of life, and God is the extender of life if He so chooses to do it. Your worries are over when you are willing to give your life you will never set your house in order as long as you're depending on your pride, your position, your bank account, your heritage, your friendships, or your intellect. You will continue to operate in your flesh.

However, when you realize that there is nothing you can do, you'll begin to set your house in order. It's a terrible thing when you have to come to that place. I thought my house was in pretty good shape, but as I began to think about the possibility of dying, I found that it wasn't. For example, I found that I had a will that was twenty years old—before we had four children. So I updated my will. I also began to realize that the world and the physical realm are fleeting, and that all that really count in this life are the relationships I had. Setting your house in order means taking care of the practical things such as a will, but it also means taking time with those who mean the most to you. Parents, spend some time with your children. Husband and wife, spend some time together. Friends, you ought to spend more time together. Chasing that commission, chasing that account, chasing that success ladder—forget it. You're better off setting your house in order in regards to what's important to God, because those are the only things that are going to count when it's all over.

When We Face the Reality of Judgment

I want to suggest to you that Ahithophel not came to understand the futility of himself, but he also came to the reality of judgment. He suddenly realized that Absalom wasn't going to be king after all. He realized that he had betrayed David, for whom he had prophesied and counseled over the years, and had all but given David into the hand of Absalom. Now his counsel had not been taken, and whether by Absalom or by David, he was sure to come under the hand of judgment. People don't set their house in order until they come to the realization that they're going to be judged by the King. I've got some happy, glorious Gospel news for you: Jesus has already paid the price for your sin! He's already become the victor! That means that judgment has been placed upon Him, that He is going to come to you and take you right where you are and set you free. But you have to face that judgment in your mind first, or you'll never do anything about it.

HOW DOES A PERSON SET HIS HOUSE IN ORDER?

How do you do this? Let's get down to brass tacks. Some of you need to do it today. How do you set your house in order? What did Ahithophel do? The scripture says that he went out and hanged himself, and he died and was buried in his father's sepulcher.

He Chooses Death

If I were going to be truly biblical, I'd say that you must first **choose to die,** but not the kind of death Ahithophel died. Do you know what the Lord showed me? He said, "George, if you'll just go ahead and die now and get it over with, we won't have to worry about anything else." If you'll just say, "Lord, that wife, those children, they are yours. I just give them to you. If I don't come out of that surgery, it doesn't really make any difference, the world soon forgets." You know, we have funerals, people die, and the world forgets you in about thirty days or less, mostly less, with the exception of the family. A few short paragraphs ago, I referred to my father, who died years ago. I'll never forget it, because he was a vital part of my life. If I live to be 120 years of age, I'll always remember him and I'll remember that experience. I remember more today than I did then because of my experience with bypass surgery. I had the same condition that eventually took his life, and had it not been for the progress of medical science, my life would have gone the same way because of a hereditary problem. Because of that, it's fresh upon my mind, but the world doesn't know him, nor will they know me. Oh, there are four children, and a wife, and a mother who would miss me, but even my congregation would quickly move on after my passing. A pulpit committee would be organized after the funeral and in less than a year's time I would have been well replaced by somebody God would have raised up, and in a few years I would be nothing more than a picture on a page and a paragraph in the church history. You see, we are soon forgotten.

Beloved, how in the world do you come to the place where you get your house in order? Let me tell you what you do: **You just die**, to start. You just give it all to God. Just say, "Lord, I'm as good as dead because I can't stay here one day longer than You intend for me to. These children belong to you. That wife belongs to you. This church belongs to you. Everything I have belongs to you. I don't have anything. I'll just go out here and "hang myself"—reckon myself dead unto the Lord Jesus Christ, for me to live is Christ, and nothing more. To die is gain."

If we could have a few good funerals, we could turn the church into a dynamo that the world couldn't handle. Are you dead to yourself? You're not hurting if you're dead to yourself. Dead folks don't hurt. People ask me how I got well so fast. It's only because I died to myself before I went in there and got that all over with. When I woke up, I had to write on a tablet for twelve hours because my mouth had been clamped shut. I've never been quiet for twelve hours in my life! A little nurse came and looked me over. She said, "Now, Mr. Harris, you're going to be like this for a few hours. You've got a thing in your mouth (like I didn't know it). Does your head hurt?" I nodded my head in a fog, and kept trying to tell her to put something under my head to prop me up, because I needed to see what was going on. Finally, I motioned for something to write on. She came over and looked at me. She was the prettiest redhead, and I just wrote on the tablet, "Are you an angel, and is this heaven?" She started laughing. She'd never seen an idiot come out of surgery like that asking questions. For twelve hours we just wrote back and forth. "Are you saved?" I would write. "What's that?" She would ask. We had a great, glorious time. You know why? I figured if I was going to be there, I might as well make the most of it. But I had to reckon that ahead of time. I want to tell you, it's scary going into surgery and not knowing if you're going to make it, but when you just decide it's all His to start with, and you just decide you're going to go out here and hang it all—give it all to Jesus, reckon yourself dead—God begins to do some things in your life you'd never believe.

That's what Ahithophel did: he just simply went out and hanged himself. Mind you, he didn't do it the right way—he did it all physically—but the parallel is the same. When you come to the place of desperation, then just die to it and give it to God, He's been standing around all eternity wanting to help, so just turn it over to Him.

I was to get rid of it. That doesn't mean that I got some kind of eternal light just because I got a bypass. God said, "I just bought you more track, but I didn't slow the train down." I'm still going in the same direction, and that's death. However, that doesn't bother me because I took care of it when I died to myself. I just said, "Lord, it's all yours. The church is yours. My family is yours. I am yours as though I do not exist and I want to reckon it so."

Beloved, that's how you begin to set your house in order. That means that the car you drive, the clothes you wear, the house you live in, the children you support, the wife you live with—none of those things belong to you. They belong to Him. When you give it all to Him, He then says, "Well, since it all belongs to me, I'm going to let you live in that house anyway. You're going to have the responsibility of those children. That money is mine but I'm going to let you take care of it. It's all mine. You're dead, as though you don't exist, but you're going to live for me and be a steward of it all. Therefore, I'm going to turn it over to you for another thirty years or so, and let you live and serve God, and then give an account for it." You have not only reckoned yourself dead, but you have also come to recognize the Lordship of Jesus Christ.

He declares the Lordship of Jesus Christ

Truly setting your house in order does not mean simply making a will (as important as that is), getting a physical, or making sure you've got all your insurance paid up. You ought to take care of those things, but what you really need to do is to be sure that you have dealt seriously with the Lord Jesus Christ; that you have made him not only the Savior of your life in case you die, but you have also made Him the Lord of all *in case you live*. You're not ready to live until you have prepared to die. When you're prepared to die, go ahead and reckon it so, and then you live for Him.

The last Sunday that I was in the hospital, which was the worst day I had physically, one of my surgeons came by the room. He stayed in my room for 2 ½ hours, and we began to talk. I had talked with him previously, and in that conversation he had told me about his pilgrimage from theism and humanism to the things of the Lord. When he came into my hospital room, he leaned up against the wall and said, "Well, Pastor, how are you feeling today?" I said, "Fine." Then I engaged him in conversation about his Christian faith.

He said, "Well, I hope someday to be able to call myself a Christian. I'm trying to learn. I started some two years ago when my boy became a Christian. I began to read some of C.S. Lewis's books. I began to read 'Evidence That Demands a Verdict' because I had a great problem with Jesus and the resurrection. I've just started praying to the Father.

"I recently had an experience that showed me that God is alive in this world today. About a year ago, I was called to the Nix Hospital to assist a man who was a cancer specialist who had diagnosed a cancer in the chest cavity of one of his patients. It was a rather large growth right next to heart, and they wanted a heart surgeon to come. I went to see the patient, and he said, 'Doctor, don't worry about me, I'm a Christian, I know the lord Jesus, and if I live, I live, and if I die, I die. All things are all right. My house is in order, I'm ready.' I came out of there thinking what a dynamic faith this man had. We didn't operate, but chose rather to start chemotherapy for six months. Six months later they called me back and said, 'It's time now; we must operate.' I went back that night for the pre-operative visit wondering if that man's faith now was greater or lesser. He had suffered so for those six months. I went to his room and, sure enough, he had dissipated a great deal. He was sick. He was tired from the chemotherapy and the lingering illness, but his faith hadn't wavered. He said to me, 'Doc, I had a dream about you last night.' I said, 'Oh, you did?' He said, 'Yes, I dreamed that you performed the surgery on me and when you made the incision into my chest it was simple enough on the surface. You could see that growth, and you began to operate, and as you began that which was simple became more complex, and that which was complex became rather severe, and that which was severe all of the sudden became impossible. You found yourself deep into that chest cavity with a tumor that was inoperable. Nothing could be done. But suddenly from heaven came a pair of illuminated hands, and they came down and merged into your gloves and lifted out that cancer.' I said to him, 'My, that was some dream!'

The next day the man was put to sleep, and I made the incision. As I began to operate, I found that which had once been the size of a grapefruit was now the size of a lemon, simple enough procedure. I began to lift it up but as I lifted I realized that it had put its tentacles into the heart sac. I had to make an opening of the heart sac. When I got the heart sac opened, all of the sudden I could see that there were tentacles all over, growing into the heart, with two great nodules growing on the aorta as the heart pumped away. I realized there was no way I'd be able to get it. I called the cancer man in and said, 'You must look at this because there is no way I can get it. We don't have a heart-lung machine in this hospital to put the man on. There's just nothing I can do.' The cancer doctor said, 'I'll tell the family,' and went out to tell the family that it was inoperable. I reached up, pushed on that nodule growing into the aorta and I pressed on one and then the other. I thought I'd just look, and I took the scalpel and lifted it just a bit to see what would happen. As I did, the tumor came up like a piece of moss on a log or a tree. It just peeled up and lifted up every one of those tentacles—everything came off until it was clean. It all came in one fell swoop. I called the other doctor back in. He looked at it, and said, "I can't believe it. It just came out!'

"George, that patient is alive in this city today. I came away knowing that there's got to be more to this business than just a Supreme Being. There's got to be personality and power. I hope someday I'll be able to say that I'm a Christian. I'm going in that direction."

I said to him, "Doctor, you've been praying all this time to know the Father. You've been talking about Jesus. I want to talk to you, not like a heart surgeon, but like a man on the street—just an ordinary man. Do you realize that you've sinned?"

He replied, "Yes."

I said, "Do you realize Jesus Christ died on the cross to pay the sin death?"

"I guess I do believe that now."

"Do you believe if you will confess with your mouth the Lord Jesus that He would come into your heart and He would live if you ask Him to do so?"

"Yes, I believe that."

I said, "Would you be willing right now just to pray that prayer?"

He thought for a minute, and then said, "You know, I guess I would have to say to you I have done that. When I get up every morning I spend a quiet time with God, and I like what has happened to me over these past two years."

I said, "Well then, who have you told?"

"Nobody."

I said, "Doc, if you would make a profession of your faith publicly and confess with your mouth that the Lord Jesus Christ is your Savior, would you let me pray for you? Would you just come over here and take my hand and let me pray for you?"

He bounded off that wall and extended his hand. I feebly got up out of my chair and stood as straight as I ever have in my life, as painful as it's ever been in my life, and put my arm around him and prayed and thanked God for this most unusual experience of a man coming to Jesus—not down the church altar, not through a soul winner, but just through a man who hungered for the things of God who said, "God, somehow out there, Father, if you're out there, reveal to me the Lord Jesus." And over a two-year pilgrimage, God began to set his house in order, until finally, one day, he said, "A few years ago I would never have humbled myself before a man or anyone else, but you know, I like the fact the Father is in control of everything."

Folks, that's what it means to get your house in order. Will you turn it over to Him and trust it to Him? Is your house in order? The tragedy is that if you don't set it in order now and you ignore the danger signs, the day may very easily come when life is taken away from you without warning, and that which you have postponed doing is too late. Your life and your existence are too precious in the sight of God for you to tamper with saying, "I'll wait, I'll wait, and I'll wait." Hebrews 9:27 says, "It is appointed for men to die once, but after this the judgment." Don't set your house in order just because it's evident that one day you're going to die. Set your house in order because it's a privilege to let Him live in you, to belong to Him as though you are already dead, and to live in victory as He merges his life into yours.

Bridges built before they are needed offer great comfort in the time of need!

CHAPTER EIGHT

DON'T QUIT NOW

A few weeks ago, one of my young grandsons came to his mother after a particularly exasperating practice and announced that he was finished with football. "Mom," he said, "Don't sign me up for baseball next year, and don't sign me up for football either, and don't sign me up for basketball." He paused for a moment, and then looked at her and said, "Don't sign me up for school, either."

There are times when we all would just like to quit. How many times have you read the want ads in the paper, wondering if there was something you could do besides what you are doing? A 1991 survey showed that 90% of all pastors work more than 46 hours a week, and that 80% believe the pastoral ministry has negatively affected their families. Over 75% report a significant stress crisis at least once in their ministry and 90% felt that they were inadequately trained to cope with ministry demands. 70% do not have anyone they could consider a close friend. Is it any wonder that ministers have times when they want to quit?

Do you realize that whole denominations also quit? They quit and don't even know it. A recent survey shows that old-line denominations begin to decline when they abandon the ideals that brought them into existence. Unaware of the shift in values, they begin to major on things other than their original purpose.

As Baptists, we have always majored on winning souls. Missions and church building have always been at the heart of our existence. Those churches that have substituted programs and events find themselves declining, and, in effect, they quit.

Paul's letter to the Philippians is one of the most evangelistic letters in the New Testament. In the Greek text, there are over 150 words that relate to battle. The most prominent recurring words are *pursue* and *apprehend.* And the word used for *work* is one that speaks of "battle." In the passage in Philippians 3, Paul admonishes his readers to keep on "pursuing," "to press on," "to apprehend just as you were apprehended." He gives us three good reasons to keep on instead of quitting.

DON'T QUIT NOW, BECAUSE THERE IS TOO MUCH TO BE GAINED IN THE FUTURE

Brethren, I do not count myself to have apprehended; but one thing I do, forgetting those things which are behind and reaching forward to those things which are ahead, I press toward the goal for the prize of the upward call of God in Christ Jesus. Philippians 3:13-14

The future demands we take inventory

In verse 13, Paul uses the Greek word *logizomai*, translated "count." From it, we get our word "logic" and it means, "to study it through." He also uses the military term "apprehended." "In thinking this thing through, I do not count myself to have apprehended," is the idea. He feels there is much yet to do in terms of taking the enemy. Have we won the battle? The answer is "No!" There is still much we must look at as we take inventory of our churches and ourselves.

In taking inventory we must *forget the past*. Paul writes, "Forgetting those things which are behind." That means *forgetting successes*. We cannot live in the past. In 2000, it was my privilege to visit England and Wales. While in Wales, I visited the little school where the Welsh Revival began under the preaching of Evan Roberts. Later the same day, I visited the Wales Bible School, started by Samuel Howell's father, who was converted under the ministry of Evan Roberts. Samuel Howell is now 93 years of age. He invited us in and treated us to tea. He also talked to us for an hour or more about the Great Revival. Things haven't changed much since 1904. The school, once known around the world for its mission emphasis, now has nine students. Long ago they lost the fire and now they are living on the memories of the past as though they will take care of the future.

A few years ago, I read a newspaper article entitled, "Is There Life After High School?" It described people whose finest hour was as Homecoming Queen, or captain of the football team. Now, 30 years later, they are 100 pounds heavier, but still living in the afterglow of those successful high school years. They haven't gone on in life to accomplish very much more. Their whole identity is wrapped up in a memory.

There are churches like that, still living in the "good old days" when Brother So-and-So could do no wrong. With the glory days behind them, they fail to recognize the good pastor and the good days in the present.

The future demands that we set some goals.

Paul used the phrase, "reaching forward to those things which are ahead, I press toward the goal . . . ." The idea of "press" is the military term "pursue in order to apprehend." Our goal and our reason for existence as a denomination are to apprehend people for Christ. When we do disaster relief, it is to win people to Christ. When we do campus retreats, it is to win collegians to Christ. When we do Sunday school growth conferences, it is to win souls to Christ. Money and numbers are significant only as they translate into souls won for Christ. God forbid that we should ever become a bureaucratic entity comfortable with our institutions and develop into a religious subculture that does not major on evangelism.

DON'T QUIT NOW BECAUSE THERE IS TOO MUCH OF THE PAST TO BE LOST

Therefore let us, as many as are mature, have this mind; and if in anything you think otherwise, God will reveal even this to you. Nevertheless, to the degree that we have already attained, let us walk by the same rule, let us be of the same mind. Phil. 3:15-16

The past should mature us

The Greek word *teleio,* translated "mature" or "complete," refers to a grownup as opposed to a child. It is primarily referring to one's attitude. Paul is writing that it is time for the Philippians to learn some lessons from the things they had been through. Jesus used the word *teleos* on the cross, when He said, "It is finished." In this context it meant, "It is complete."

The past should motivate us

While we cannot live in the past, the experiences of the past should have matured us and should also motivate us. They should especially motivate our thinking. The phrase, "have this mind," speaks of attitude. It is an attitude of success, security, and determination based on God's previous leadership; thus we know we can count on His leadership in the future. This is reflected in the phrase, "God will reveal even this unto you."

The word used here for reveal refers to an unveiling. We must depend upon God unveiling the way before us, day-by-day, week-by-week, and year-by-year. That means our attitude must be such that we are open and subject to changes. God has promised the future to us if we follow His leadership but today's successes do not guarantee tomorrow's. To become discouraged and to quit now is to lose all that has been gained from the past.

Abraham Lincoln failed in business and was not re-elected to Congress after his successful election in 1846. In 1856, he was defeated in his bid for the vice-presidency. But in spite of the uphill battle against circumstances, he persisted until he was elected President of our country in 1860. Success came after twenty years of struggle.

Winston Churchill is another great example of perseverance. Had he died at age 65, he would have been remembered as virtually a failure. A poor student in his early years, he had a questionable military career. But after he was 65 years of age, he dared pursue the office of Prime Minister of England, an office no one seemed to want. The rest is history. He because a legend before he died in his nineties because of his leadership and his bull-headed courage during the years of the Second World War.

We can all learn from the past. Anthony Campolo, the sociologist, conducted a survey of 100 people in their nineties and asked the question: "If you had to do it over again, what would you do differently?" There were basically three answers:

1. I would dream bigger.
2. I would risk more.
3. I would spend my life doing something that would live on after I die.

DON'T QUIT NOW BECAUSE THERE IS TOO MUCH TO BE DONE IN THE PRESENT

Brethren, join in following my example, and note those who so walk, as you have us for a pattern. For many walk, of whom I have told you often, and now tell you even weeping, that they are the enemies of the cross of Christ: whose end is destruction, whose god is their belly, and whose glory is in their shame—who set their mind on earthly things. For our citizenship is in heaven, from which we also

> *eagerly wait for the Savior, the Lord Jesus Christ, who will transform our lowly body that it may be conformed to His glorious body, according to the working by which He is able even to subdue all things to Himself. (Philippians 3:17-20)*

We have an example to follow

Paul challenged the Philippian Christians to focus on the present. He went on to say, "Follow my example." The word translated "follow" also means "be imitators." It is both our personal choice and our individual responsibility to be imitators of the godly examples set before us. The word translated "note" is the Greek word *topos* from which we get our word topography. It means, "the mark caused by a blow or an impression," "a pattern," "to be impressed by those who are different from the world." It has always been interesting to me that so many Christians are impressed with those in the world and try to become like them rather than setting a godly example before them.

Our example is in contrast with the world

There has never been a day when our example of the Christian walk has been in greater contrast with the world—" . . . whose end is destruction, whose god is their belly, and whose glory is their shame; who set their minds on earthly things." The shamelessness of those who parade their shameful, sinful lives on the Jerry Springer Show and in countless other public forums is unparalleled. Our consciousness of right and wrong has been desensitized by the media bombardment of tasteless immorality.

We have an enemy to overcome

The devil has always been the enemy of the cross of Christ. Beginning in the Garden of Eden and continuing to this very day, he has sought to stand in the way of our Savior. He did his best to prevent the Incarnation, and as Christ was tempted in the wilderness, he did his best to disqualify our Savior. As Christ was laid in the tomb, he gloried in a temporary victory, but three days later, at the Resurrection, he suffered his final defeat. Today, he lives in his final hours as the prince of the air, playing out his bluff on uninformed Christians. But I am here to tell you that he is a defeated foe. In these final hours of history, he would attempt to make us shrink from our tasks and cower in fear, but we must boldly stand in the victory of the cross.

> *And they overcame him by the blood of the Lamb and by the word of their testimony, and they did not love their lives to death" (Revelation 12:11).*

We have a reward to look forward to

Our manner of living is in heaven and our eyes should be focused on a coming Lord, our fears eradicated by the promise that we are only passing through this world. "Soon and very soon" we will be transformed into His likeness.

Paul makes a point of contrast: our future bodies will not be like these we have now—full of passions and weaknesses—but our job in the present is to live with eternity in mind. Get ready for the Glory!

The word for "fashion" is the Greek word *summorphon*, which means, "to fashion anew." It is the word from which we get our word metamorphosis. It is also the same word used in

Romans 8:29 where it is translated "conform." It means an inside-out transformation, a total extreme makeover.

Paul knew that many would die for their faith, he would be one of them, and so he emphasized: "Don't quit now; there is too much to be done in this present time. God's power is able . . . remember that Jesus is Lord."

Years ago in Austria, a young marksman named Hans went to the 1954 Olympics. He stood and fired 100 rounds from his pistol. Ninety-nine of his bullets hit the bull's eye and he returned home with the gold medal for marksmanship. The next year, he toured his country as a national hero. Then he returned to the factory where he was employed. In a freak accident, his arm was caught in the machinery, and he lost his arm at the elbow. For over a year, Hans grieved his loss and descended into depression.

One day, while sitting at the breakfast table with his wife and daughter, he said to his wife, "Honey, there comes a time when a man has to do what a man has to do." He got up from the table and started out the door. His wife caught a glimpse of the handle of a pistol sticking out of his belt.

Hans crossed the road and disappeared into the forest. His wife, her emotions spiraling out of control, hurriedly followed behind him. She paused behind a tree and then heard the sound of a shot being fired, "BANG!" Her heart sank and tears began to flow as she slowly looked from behind the tree where she was hiding. Then she heard another shot, then another . . . six altogether. There stood Hans with his pistol tucked under the nub of his right arm, reloading. He continued to fire at the target as she watched in amazement.

In 1958, Hans stood once more in the marksman's box at the Olympics. Once more, this time with his left hand, he fired 100 rounds at the target, and 98 of them went into the bull's eye. Hans went home with another gold medal. Don't quit now!

I suppose President Theodore Roosevelt said it best in a speech he delivered, entitled, "It's Not the Critic That Counts:"[1]

> "It is not the critic who counts; not the man who points out how the strong man stumbles, or where the doer of deeds could have done them better. The credit belongs to the man who is actually in the arena, whose face is marred by dust and sweat and blood, who strives valiantly; who errs and comes short again and again; because there is not effort without error and shortcomings; but who does actually strive to do the deed; who knows the great enthusiasm, the great devotion, who spends himself in a worthy cause, who at the best knows in the end the triumph of high achievement and who at the worst, if he fails, at least he fails while daring greatly. So that his place shall never be with those cold and timid souls who know neither victory nor defeat."

The bridge of perseverance is the hardest to erect, but the most rewarding to cross.

END NOTES

Chapter 2

1. This is not a written word, but a part of the written word (Scripture) that God, through His Spirit, speaks to you.
2. Lexical aids to the Old Testament. The Hebrew Greek Study Bible, by Spiro Zodhiates, p. 1648.
3. Ibid, p. 1615.
4. Ibid, p. 1592.

Chapter 3

1. 2 Samuel 4:4
2. 1 Samuel 20:42; 2 Samuel 9:1
3. Matthew 28:19-20
4. Luke 19:10
5. 2 Samuel 9:3
6. Luke 19:10
7. 2 Samuel 9:11

8. Romans 8:16
9. Colossians 1:27
10. John 16:15
11. Philippians 4:13
12. Ephesians 2:8-9

Chapter 4

1. Young's Concordance, p. 338

Chapter 6

1. Webster, New Collegiate Dictionary, page 116.

Chapter 8

1. "Citizenship in a Republic," Speech at the Sorbonne, Paris, April 23, 1910

CPSIA information can be obtained
at www.ICGtesting.com
Printed in the USA
BVHW071752060222
628193BV00001B/35